OLIVE,
MABEL &
ME

OLIVE, MABEL & ME

Life and Adventures with Two Very Good Dogs

ANDREW COTTER

BLACK & WHITE PUBLISHING

First published in 2020
This edition first published 2021
by Black & White Publishing Ltd
Nautical House, 104 Commercial Street
Edinburgh EH6 6NF

5 7 9 10 8 6 4   21 22 23 24

ISBN (PBK): 978 1 78530 336 4

A CIP catalogue record for this book is available from the British Library.

Typeset by Iolaire, Newtonmore
Printed and bound by CPI Group (UK) Ltd, Croydon, CR0 4YY

MIX
Paper from
responsible sources
FSC
www.fsc.org   FSC® C171272

For good dogs everywhere

Contents

Foreword

Olive

I should be honest here and say that I initially wanted nothing to do with this book as I couldn't see how it would, in any way, benefit me – something which I feel is quite important. But then it was explained that, firstly, I would get top-billing and, secondly, the food we eat (and if you have any spare, that would be great) doesn't grow on trees. I countered by pointing out that I eat most parts of trees on a regular basis.

Eventually, though, I was sold on the idea that people might read it and subsequently tell me that I was a very good dog. Because that pleases me. So here is our story, in words that we would choose if we knew a few more of them, but since my vocabulary stretches at most to 'walk', 'biscuit' and assorted other treats, we agreed to let Andrew write it on our behalf. I did make him promise to describe us only in glowing terms and he said he would, although at the time he was crossing his fingers in a way that I could only envy.

I have no idea why we have seen far more of him recently (which also pleases me), or why so many people are stopping us on our walks to say hello, or why he seems to be filming us more often than usual. I just know that whatever success we might have had, or fame we might have achieved, is entirely down to me.

But, in the end, I am sure that we will come out of the book well.
Because I know he loves me a lot and – please don't tell him – I
really am quite fond of him too.

Mabel
Which one is Andrew again?

Cheshire, October 2020

Prologue

31st December 2019

Torridon, in the north-west of Scotland, provides a landscape like no other. Rolling miles of peat and heather, studded by a thousand lochs and pools, out of which rise giant and solitary mountains.

An Teallach is perhaps the finest of them all – a sharp and imposing wedge of sandstone which can appear a fiery red in a low sun. Hence the name which, in English, means the forge, or hearth.

For the past three hours it had been rather more feebly illuminated by a head torch as we made our way up the northern slopes from the edge of Little Loch Broom. But then, the winter night, so long at this time of year, finally began to loosen its grip. We could see the sky in the east lighten and silhouettes of other peaks started to form as we climbed the final slopes to the summit – and by the time we reached the ridge the faintest glow had become the most glorious sunrise lifting above the horizon. It was a beautiful place to see dawn on the final day of the year, from the top of one of Scotland's most dramatic mountains. I was utterly captivated by the sight. The remaining members of the expedition were facing the other way and sniffing at something small and recently deceased.

So that's us: Olive, Mabel and me – companions on many walks and in life in general. Eventually they gathered round, tempted in by bits of cheese and mini-sausages and, as we sat together, I thought about how much they meant to me and that I was glad I had them here. Climbing mountains has always been an escape – it is for most people who head for the hills and certainly is for me. Getting away from the occasional madness of the world below, more often than not accompanied by my dogs.

Up on the ridge of An Teallach the three of us were offered the most incredible panorama. Behind us, to the west, the sky above the sea was still dark, but we were looking forward as the sun continued its own reluctant climb. A new year was nearly with us and I wondered what it might bring.

I wanted to stay far longer, but it was bitterly cold. And in any case the views were once again not being fully appreciated by either of my assistants, who continued to forage in the never-ending Labrador quest for food – Olive now pawing optimistically at a bit of moss in the frozen ground, Mabel striking a rather richer vein within my rucksack.

So we turned and headed back. Back down to the other world and all the life and chaos and noise that it brings. With my two dogs trotting behind, none of us with any idea quite how chaotic and strange this particular new year would be.

1. Game Gone, Game On

When asked to name your favourite year, I'm not sure that 2020 would be high on anybody's list. The CEO of Zoom might disagree, perhaps sailing around the Caribbean on his yacht pulled by a fleet of swans. But almost everybody else who has lived through it will have very distinct memories of the deep unpleasantness – lockdown, lost jobs, strained relationships and even worse. And above all, the overriding *oddness* as our lives were utterly transformed by a global pandemic. For me, that feeling was only heightened by something I brought upon myself in the spring, as

I somehow fashioned our entirely unwitting Labradors, Olive and Mabel, into viral stars of the internet.

In my normal job (which, admittedly, is not particularly normal) I am a sports broadcaster – commentating on all manner of events, mainly for the BBC, but really for anybody who will employ me. It is a hugely enjoyable profession and one that I am very fortunate to do – travelling around, describing the action in golf, rugby, tennis, athletics and other major events besides. But it does rather depend on sport actually taking place, which has never been an issue. Until this strange year of 2020.

It was during the Six Nations rugby tournament – one of the highlights of my working calendar – when we started to feel that things were perhaps going slightly amiss. A couple of events had already been cancelled because of the coronavirus which was moving across from Asia into Europe and beyond. Matches in Italy and Ireland were now being called off and there were murmurings of far worse to come. In early March, French authorities also decided to put a ban on mass gatherings and their final game was postponed. By the entirely appropriate date of Friday the 13th, only one fixture was left standing – Wales against Scotland. I was due to commentate and was getting ready to set off for Cardiff when the texts and emails started arriving.

'Game gone. Give me a call,' came the short, slightly harassed message from the editor. Two minutes later, an email arrived from Augusta National Golf Club: 'Unfortunately we have decided at this time to postpone the Masters Tournament . . .' and this was quickly followed by the disappearance of the London Marathon – which would seem quite a thing to mislay. And so the sporting house of cards started to collapse. Event after event was being called off and it didn't escape my notice that being a freelance sports commentator with no sport occurring anywhere in the world might prove tricky.

Of course, for most people in that position their immediate thought will be, 'Can I pay bills and the mortgage?' And yes, this did cross my mind. How my next thought came to be, 'Well ... perhaps I should commentate on my dogs eating their breakfast and then put it on Twitter' I'm still not quite sure.

That said, ego is a fairly strong suspect – the firm belief that other people *very* much need to hear your voice and listen to your opinions or, indeed, that you like to try and make people laugh. These are traits which will probably be found more in broadcasters than other members of the human race, but most people have them to a certain extent. That, after all, is what fuels social media – feeling the need to share. So, on that fateful day, suddenly jobless, I went out, iPhone in hand, the dogs questioning why I was looking for a more scenic location than their usual feeding spot by the washing machine and the slightly grubby skirting-board. Although for them it was just another offering of food and they would eat it by the bins if necessary. They would then try to eat from the bins. But on this occasion they certainly wouldn't have cared or noticed that I was beside them, filming as they ate and offering a little bit more chat during their meals than I normally do.

And that was it. Although, in fact, I sat on the video for a couple of weeks. Not initially convinced that it was riotously amusing anyway, and I tended to live by the Twitter rule, 'If in doubt, just don't do it.' But in those next weeks, my working diary emptied entirely: the Boat Race, Wimbledon, the Tokyo Olympics and the Open Championship were either postponed or cancelled. So I was left at a very loose end. 'I was bored' as I wrote in the tweet which I finally decided to release into the wilds of the internet.

One click and it all began.

2. Bored Game

I like to think that I am used to a reasonable amount of attention. Through my work I have a small profile which means that once in a while people outside my close friends and family might know who I am. Occasionally in the past I might even have put out a tweet that gave two or three people the urge to type 'LOL!'. But what I was about to experience was on an entirely different level.

'I think your Twitter might be going a bit mad,' said my partner Caroline, after just a few minutes. Indeed, Olive and Mabel eating, with a bit of commentary thrown in, already had thousands of views, likes, retweets. Very quickly it managed to leave far behind any occasion when I might have made a cutting yet brilliant observation about Tiger Woods.

Caroline was keeping a keen eye on proceedings and shouting through, at fairly regular intervals, some notables who had retweeted it. Rattling off names as if running down a list of potential guests for a mid-morning chat show.

'Gary Lineker . . . Simon Mayo . . . Dara Ó Briain . . . Kirstie Allsopp . . .'

When something goes viral on the internet the fascinating thing is how it spreads. You can see it happen and chart its progress. Those shouted names then became a live commentary on the video's movement from domestic to international.

'Toby and Josh from *The West Wing* have retweeted.'

'RYAN REYNOLDS!!!!' texted a friend, as I sat watching television, eating cereal and feigning disinterest in the cyber-wildfire. Head to Twitter and yes, there is Deadpool himself offering a quote from the dog-commentary and a laughing emoji. I was very close to replying with 'Thanks, Ryan! LOVED *La La Land*!!' but realised just in time my Ryan-based confusion.

It had also been picked up by ESPN and by Buzzfeed – huge Twitter accounts which accelerated the spread. One million . . . two million . . . three million views. The counter whirred. 'Damn . . . I had Mabel!' tweeted Ron Perlman aka 'Hellboy' of those films, as our virus appeared to be hitting superheroes particularly hard.

It seemed strange to me how much this tweet was being appreciated in the United States. In my head, the humour of it was in a semi-recognisable sports broadcaster turning his hand to something utterly mundane. But in America nobody would be aware of who I was or what I did. In fact, there were a significant number of comments expressing the idea that I should try to become a professional sports announcer because 'You sound just like one'.

The reaction was extraordinary. Every morning I was waking up to messages and emails of appreciation from the furthest reaches of the globe. Every day brought dozens of requests for interviews. Initially – suddenly a novice in the ways of the media once more – you say yes to them, because . . . well, why not? Then you realise that this is only the start and you probably should have paced yourself. Skypes, FaceTimes and Zooms followed with the *Telegraph*, the *Guardian*, CBS, ABC, even Kennel Club TV in America. There were chats on radio stations in Australia, New Zealand, Ireland, South Africa and Canada. And countless other enquiries which had to be turned down. The world was suddenly looking in on and sharing our two dogs, who remained blissfully ignorant of the clamour, as indeed they are about most things.

At that point this odd little video, which I very nearly didn't bother uploading, had racked up somewhere around eight million views. Once you're past a few thousand views, the figures become harder to comprehend. But this number is somewhere in the region of the population of London. And then there are the other numbers – the 'followers' as they are called on social media, with hints of religious fervour.

The faithful flock of my Twitter account had been not small, but certainly not Kardashian in scale and was operating around the 45,000 mark. Bear in mind that this had been accrued over a period of eleven years, during which my work as a broadcaster had given me some interest from people who were keen on the various sports which I covered. But the diversity of my portfolio probably didn't help – some might have drifted in thinking that I would tweet about golf and drifted quickly out again when a rugby tweet appeared. Likewise tennis or athletics fans came and went through the revolving door when they realised I mostly posted pictures of mountains, or links to videos on YouTube of pets falling over.

Besides, before Olive and Mabel took off, my interest in and fondness for Twitter had all but disappeared. I had been a fairly early adopter, back in 2009, and it seemed to be a friendlier, more enjoyable place then. Somewhere you could be a bit silly and have some fun, all with the feeling of an entertaining sideshow.

With the rise in the popularity of Twitter came a change in its tone. More people joined and more serious matters were discussed – and by 'discussed' we of course generally mean people shouting abuse at each other from opposing sides of the arguments. Silly and fun had been replaced by criticism and outrage. It quickly morphed into a far more divisive place than the unifying, agreeable and altogether pleasant force it was probably designed to be.

Also, as a broadcaster, I became well aware that you had to put up with a certain amount of feedback on Twitter. In decades past if somebody watched an event where they were upset by a commentator – if a mistake had been made or they strongly disagreed with something you had said and they desperately felt the urge to tell you, then it would have involved a lot of effort on their part. Get a piece of paper and a pen, write down the all-important critique, then find an envelope and a stamp and track down the relevant address at the BBC before heading to the postbox. Then sit back for a couple of days, possibly fuming at some other stuff on TV or life in general and wonder if your letter was ever read by any human eyes.

With the advent of social media – and in particular Twitter – the process was almost immediate. From disagreement, to rage, to typing angry thoughts and pressing send. Received by your target and all done and dusted in just a few seconds.

My safeguard against such correspondence was to simply deactivate my account before commentating on a major sporting event. I wish I had done so when providing the commentary for the BBC on the opening ceremony at the 2016 Olympic Games in Rio de Janeiro. Not that I said anything controversial or incorrect at all, but it's impossible to give the history of all 207 countries trooping into the Maracanã Stadium without upsetting somebody, somewhere. Draw attention to the fact that a certain nation didn't compete in the Games until 1972 because before that it had still been under the control of a colonial power and you would suffer the wrath of the Twitter righteous:

'Jeez . . . @mrandrewcotter seems to be longing for the days of empire . . .' was a fairly standard message that greeted me on the way back to the hotel.

Curiously, tennis often seemed to prompt the fiercest backlash, from the dedicated fans of whichever player you were commentating on – those devoted to the big three of Roger Federer, Rafa Nadal and Novak Djokovic were particularly vocal and if you didn't offer constant gushing praise throughout one of their matches, you would fear the worst when switching your phone on afterwards.

'I hope you die of a really virulent form of cancer' was one from a Djokovic fan which sticks in the memory, after we had mentioned during the second set that he was struggling with his forehand.

There's no doubt that there was still plenty that was good and entertaining about Twitter and social media in general – you could find links to some very funny content popping up in your time-line. And, of course, it could be used to receive a feed of news or interesting stories. But then, if you only follow like-minded people, which is the way most of us operate, you tend to be only seeing things from your own viewpoint.

We are constantly told that the world is more connected than ever, as if this is an amazing gift for our generation, but it also means that the unpleasant side of human nature can spread as quickly as the good and that the divisions become more obvious. I would constantly long to be rid of Twitter – to just get off the grid, switch off and escape. But then you are told, by those in the know, that in the media industry you simply *must* have a social media presence – in particular if you are self-employed because the business is, to a certain extent, about self-promotion. Another part of life and work with which I've never felt comfortable.

So I kept my Twitter account alive, but only barely and with no real enthusiasm for it. And that's where I was – treading water, but not particularly interested in trying to swim – when the Olive and Mabel wave hit.

As mentioned, very quickly that first video had a London-sized number of views. Accompanying that was a commuter-town's worth of new followers. Having climbed slowly and steadily over eleven years to get to 45,000, that figure now shot up to 90,000 within just a few days. In a way it was quite humbling – over a decade of occasional, pithy remarks about life and sport in 140 characters or fewer, matched by one tweet of dogs eating.

The other remarkable thing – given the breakdown in my relationship with Twitter, citing irreconcilable differences – was that, in this little corner of the app at least, things were pleasant and polite again. People were still messaging in their thousands and, strangely for this tainted social medium, they were all positive.

How nice, I thought, as I prepared to get back to doing other things – returning to whatever it was I had been concerned with before this video happened and content to think of it as a one-off.

Perhaps something to be laughed about in years to come, remembering 'that Olive and Mabel viral thing'.

But then I started noticing that while the messages about the video were all grateful and generous and kind, a huge number of them also contained a question.

'When's the next one out?'

3. Game of Bones

Another video had most assuredly not been part of the plan. I know this because there wasn't a plan, but as the days passed the calls for a follow-up only increased.

I like to imagine that this is what happens when a film has major success. The directors or actors are kicking back, having worked for months on their cherished project. It's all in the can, the premiere is a hit and the box-office takings are good. So enjoy the glow and settle down for a well-deserved repose on the laurels. Then comes the call from the studio executives. '*Nice*, guys. Need that sequel now . . .'

I didn't really want to go anywhere near a sequel, even if it was just a minute-long video of dogs, which admittedly would take slightly less time and effort to put together than *The Empire Strikes Back*. My concern was that there was no way it would reach the audience or have the success of the first one. What if it wasn't as good? Less *Godfather Part II* and more *Police Academy 7: Mission to Moscow*.

With films you know how successful they've been through various means: box-office takings, critical response, etc. There might be no ticket price charged on a tweet, but you still have plenty of data to let you know how it has performed.

I should add that sports broadcasters live in a world of statistics and numbers – they are the measure of success for a player or team. So here are some Twitter stats for you on that first video . . .

> *Dog's Breakfast (season so far)*
> Views: 10.4 million
> Retweets: 112,000
> Likes: 350,000
> Comments: 9,300
> Resulting interview requests: 120 (approx)

Put like that, you can see that the pressure was building. However, reaching for analogy into another art form, we were experiencing, as one of my colleagues put it, 'the difficult second album'.

Fortunately, Olive and Mabel felt no such pressure and delivered within a couple of weeks, emerging from their enormous trailers complete with mini-bars and satellite television and deciding to have a slow, tension-filled tussle over one of their well-chewed toys. There was certainly good fortune in how it played out, with the two of them nailing their parts. Olive losing control of the rubber bone and looking, with all the sadness a Labrador can muster, into the camera at the end. Great drama and pathos, I thought, while pausing only briefly to reflect on the fact that dog-commentary was apparently my life now. But this one I felt sure would get a decent reaction.

And how . . .

Within a few minutes 'Game of Bones' as it became known, had taken off. If the first one was catching, the second was a new super-virulent strain. Within an hour it was doing what the first one had achieved in a day. But, like the original, it was the sheer variety of people from all countries and all walks of life who were sharing it that was remarkable. And once more some friends were celebrity-spotting.

'LUKE SKYWALKER!!' came a brief and to the point message on WhatsApp.

A quick check and yes, there was Mark Hamill passing it on to his millions of followers on Twitter and Instagram. Some basketball-loving acquaintances in California texted me in quite an excited fashion to relay the news that Steve Kerr loved the play-by-play. A quick tap into Google was necessary to reveal that he's the coach of the Golden State Warriors. In fact, I saw him recently in the Netflix documentary about Michael Jordan, as they played together for the great Chicago Bulls side. Each time he appeared on screen I would scratch the ear of whichever dog was beside me on the sofa and whisper, 'That guy there pounding the three-pointers? Big fan of yours.'

Back on the domestic front there was reaction from people who have made a career in comedy, which somehow made it even more gratifying. Rory Bremner, Kevin Bridges, Adrian Edmondson. Then the great God of Satire himself, Armando Iannucci, expressed his approval.

Once again the media latched on to it, probably even more so than the first. Over the next week we saw Mabel's rather hapless yet endearing face staring out at us from *The Times* and Matt Lucas was introducing the clip on Channel 4. Requests came in from Breakfast Television on BBC and ITV. The evening news on MSNBC in the United States ended with the video and with anchor Brian Williams saying, 'Good night and thanks . . . to the great Olive and Mabel.'

All of this seemed extraordinary to me, but probably demonstrated a couple of things – firstly, how all feelings intensified at that time. Emotions, both good and bad, were heightened in a time of lockdown. And people just wanted to laugh at something – they wanted a distraction from lives which were becoming quite stressful. With nothing else to do and no place else to go, people were also living more and more on social media. I know that I was. Usually with a job and other things to focus upon, social media is a side issue, perhaps glanced at for a few spare minutes, sometimes not at all. But now it had become far more central to the lives of a lot of people. Apart from anything else, I wouldn't have made the video clips in our usual, 'normal' lives and they probably wouldn't have been taken to in quite the same way. It seemed that they had just captured the oddness of the time and the feeling that we all needed some sort of whimsical diversion.

The popularity of them was also driven by the fact that people simply love their dogs and, during those weird weeks and months, our canine companions were needed more than ever. Dogs offer therapy at the best of times and now, in some of the worst, they really stepped up. I would suggest that if there is some sort of bonus scheme then dogs should be getting an enormous cheque after everything we've been through. Or, at the very least, an extra biscuit. Not that they did anything different you understand – they just carried on being dogs, oblivious to the greater cares and stresses of the world. Happy enough with a regular supply of food, a walk now and again and somewhere comfortable to doze at regular intervals.

In the meantime, my Twitter account had exploded in size and transformed in genre, from a sports-dominated following to a huge assembly who wanted more dog-based antics.

Let's return, once again, to the sporting stats-book:

> *Game of Bones (season so far)*
> Views: 19.7 million
> Retweets: 221,000
> Likes: 671,000
> Comments: 14,000

In fact, if I now tweeted anything that wasn't in some way connected to dogs, I was quickly put in my place. 'Um . . . I don't really care about golf. Olive and Mabel please?'

'Really? Another one?' came the questions from my inner voice, but of course I knew the reply.

'Well, yes, don't you get it? You've created a monster. And once you start feeding it, the monster will always want more.'

4. Pond Life and Penguins

A confession – I am weak and easily swayed by public opinion. Therefore I caved to the demands and a third video followed.

Although, put like that, it sounds so easy – as if another idea had simply fallen from the skies, or that I summoned it on tap from the dark depths of my head. But, in reality, the creative process had been agony. I always laughed – but in a sad and bitter fashion – when the message came in asking for another video, with various people even suggesting I should make it a daily thing. A *daily* video? Did they have no idea what was involved? The thought and the time that was required to make a ninety-second video was far more than some seemed to appreciate. Also, I had got lucky with the second one in terms of content but still, in came the demands for 'More more MORE!!' and the inspiration-free days rolled by and turned into a couple of weeks.

'Where are Olive and Mabel?' was a standard enquiry that hit my inbox. These were usually nice enough, but sometimes also illustrated with a GIF of a sulking child or a cat looking really pissed off.

Again, I would love to say that I wasn't bothered – that I was quite sanguine about the whole thing and that these people would just have to wait for the next one. Hey, I would casually shrug . . . there might not even be a next one. No worries at all . . . I'm fine with that . . . not a problem . . .

But as I said, I am weak and deeply crave the approval of total strangers. I was also in the slightly needy zone of feeling that I had to live up to the expectations of the famous people who had been in touch. My vivid and quite troubled imagination ran wild with the notion that Ryan Reynolds was sitting in his Malibu Beach house, refreshing his Twitter feed and furrowing his brow, before deciding to let his own sixteen million followers know what he thought.

'Still nothing new from @mrandrewcotter. And I thought he was a cool guy . . . #shame.'

Every day I would be thinking of what I could do. A common event which kept appearing in my own Twitter feed (as I now seemed to be a lightning rod for all things canine) was two dogs with a line of food in front of them, racing against each other to see who could finish first, to all-round hilarity. But that wasn't really the point of the Olive and Mabel videos. It wasn't about contriving a situation, or about engineering a sporting contest between the two. The whole concept so far had been dogs just being dogs – doing very normal and mundane dog things, whether it be eating or playing.

That's not to say I didn't briefly try such things. Lines of food were carefully laid out in our garden. I acted alone as Caroline wanted little to do with what she, quite rightly, felt was an increasing level of insanity. I would then grow frustrated when Olive started eating before I had said 'Go!', or we had to do another take because it hadn't ended properly. Now that I think about it, Olive may have been deliberately getting things wrong.

Or I would go out on our evening walk and, whereas before I had just enjoyed throwing discs or balls for Olive and Mabel, now I was trying to create the ideal sporting contest, then getting annoyed that they hadn't delivered the perfect pay-off. What was this madness?

In the end, a moment did come on a walk and it was far better than any of those staged situations. It was, as I have said, dogs just being dogs. Mabel hopped into her favourite pond for reasons known only to her, while Olive had a little think about life a few yards away. Spot the appeal, quickly press record and think about what to say . . .

By now I was a little bit unsure about it all and the inner voice of doubt spoke up. 'Mabel's doing nothing in this video, so why would people be interested or find it funny?' My nerve had gone. Now in my head I was cutting to Armando Iannucci's house, as he shouted through to his family, 'Another video from Cotter – but *Christ* he's lost it. I'm actually embarrassed for him.' So I gently pressed send on a soft release late at night on Instagram, thinking that if only my mother and sympathetic friends approve, I'll delete and we'll never speak of it again. But within *seconds* it received dozens of likes. Apart from anything else this did make me wonder how much of what you see on social media is down to bots, or automated accounts. There is no possible way that the initial likes had time to watch the video before the approval came. Or maybe they just really liked the opening frame.

Anyway, more genuine and complimentary reaction kept on coming, so up it went on Twitter as well and, once more, in came the love. Since I seem to be in celebrity-listing mode, Hugh Grant, Dawn French, Kathy Burke, Emily Maitlis and Sue Perkins were among those to hop on board. Again, the positives were overwhelming. The messages from so many people expressing the sentiment that the video had given them a laugh which they needed at that moment.

But for all the fun of all the videos – and, I confess, the thrill of watching them get picked up and passed around – they also cast something of a shadow. It might sound strange but the problem was because of the immutable Law of Twitter which states that 'Tweet x popularity + visible email address = inbox overload'. In the past I had had an email address on my Twitter profile because, as a freelance broadcaster, you need to be contactable in case somebody wants to offer you work. So, once in a blue moon I might get an email dropping in to ask if I were available.

Now the world flooded in. Hundreds of emails a day, every day, with all manner of queries. As well as the requests to do newspaper, TV or radio interviews, there were dozens from people who sent me videos of their pets, or of their children and suggested that I might be able to do some commentary on them. Among the countless animal antics were goats racing each other, kittens playing football and guinea-pigs fighting, dressed up in little karate outfits, and whose owners thought these 'would be perfect for your next funny video!!'.

There were, too, some genuine offers of employment – one came in from Visit Victoria, the tourism body in Australia, wondering if they might commission me to commentate on the penguins of Phillip Island, south of Melbourne. Since penguins are inherently funny and, perhaps more importantly, since I had no other income at the time, I went ahead and described the birds making their nightly waddle from sea to burrow.

It might have all seemed ridiculous, but it was in fact an example of great marketing. I later discovered that Phillip Island Nature Parks had, because of the obvious drop in tourist numbers, been heading for grim times and were contemplating laying off the vast majority of their staff. But they lobbied the Victorian Government for funding, with part of their pitch the idea for this video, and they were granted a lifeline.

It certainly helped that the video took off – at the time of writing it has had about sixty million views around the world. More and more interview requests then poured in and a significant number of them were from Australia, but since Olive and Mabel had also been a big hit there I lost track of what I was being approached about and considered starting every reply with, 'Are we talking dogs or penguins?'

The upside of it all was enormous publicity and a significant boost for a tourism and conservation body when they needed it most and, into the bargain, I was offered a giant toy penguin as a gift. I reluctantly told them that I would have to politely decline as Olive would not be at all interested in its conservation.

More often though, the suggestions for work which came in could quickly be tucked away in a file marked 'Not with a barge pole'. There was a car rental company asking if I would commentate on their vehicles being cleaned. I was offered the chance to describe the Dorset knob-eating competition (a type of bread roll apparently) and the organisers of the Beer Mile – where competitors race round a track but have to down (the official term being 'chug') a beer every four laps – thought I was just the man for the job. Then a multibillion-dollar video game company emailed to ask if I might become an e-sports announcer for them. This was intriguing until they explained that it was not for virtual golf or football or tennis, but for the leagues where teams play each other at *Call of Duty* and another game called *Overwatch*. Checking them out, both appeared to involve large amounts of death and destruction while the commentators shouted phrases which, for those not familiar with the game, made no sense at all. I suppose not unlike rugby union.

There were offers of ads – for pizza, for yoghurt, for online shopping and any number of sports-betting companies, which were all easy enough to turn down. Even in days without work I wanted to maintain some sort of standards and principles. It would have been very easy to say yes to absolutely everything for a bit of short-term income, but longer-term you might forever be remembered very differently.

More difficult were the huge numbers of people emailing to tell me their stories. Sometimes they came from those who were in very sad situations or were telling me about a family tragedy and were asking if I might be able to film a message of support. On a few occasions I did. More often I just replied saying that I hoped things got better for them. Sometimes, with the volume of requests coming in, I couldn't even do that.

The best way I can describe the feeling is as if tens of thousands of people had suddenly come to your house and started talking at you. Some of them with questions, others offering compliments, some making demands. Every one of them is being very pleasant about it, but they're still there, standing in your garden chattering away, a human version of Hitchcock's *The Birds*. After a while all I could do was draw the curtains, without so much as offering them a cup of tea.

The things is, you are aware that it's your own fault because you have effectively invited them to drop on by. But I had been given just a glimpse of some of the emotions and issues affecting people all around the world and I admit that with the slight strain I was also feeling at the time – concerned, as most of us were, about work and life in general – it wasn't particularly easy. You soak up every message and bit of information that comes in, like a sponge, until you feel rather heavy and laden down yourself. The last thing you would want to do in a situation like that is willingly put yourself through it all again. Unless, of course, you are some kind of attention-seeking fool.

5. Zoom Time

Yes, I put out another video.
   Again, it's such a short sentence, as if I just wanted to put out a video, so I did. But a huge amount of thought had gone into it. Each of the three so far had had something different about them – a fast-paced commentary, then slower style and then quirky. But now I wanted to break free from the sports commentary genre – to try something different. As with the pond one, inspiration struck while out walking Olive and Mabel, at the end of a day overloaded with Zoom calls – most of them outlining the extent to which we now

wouldn't be employed. As I watched them both careering round a field, concentrating on simple play and sheer enjoyment, so far from our own lives of structure and work and stress, it just seemed obvious – transplant them both into our world for a moment. And so I planned an online video-conference call featuring Olive and Mabel.

I was pleased with the thought of moving things on – it was a bit like a TV series which develops with time and reveals more of the characters' personality traits with each episode. Mabel showing herself here to be slightly scatty and juvenile; Olive rather more steady and dependable. Again, it was quite a simple idea, but the execution of it was a bit more complicated. I'm sure there are some people who firmly believe that I just recorded a Zoom meeting with both of my dogs. But neither Olive nor Mabel owns a laptop or has an email address. And besides, their technical competence is limited. So the vast majority will realise that a fair amount of filming and a good number of takes and decent timing was required. Then some clever production work by a colleague of mine, Tony Mabey, to create the overall effect. I have decent editing skills but he is approaching Grand Master level and the finished product looked authentic.

Even I could admit to being relatively pleased with this one, so light the blue touch-paper and stand back . . .

Except, once again, I did so with real trepidation. I wanted it to succeed and felt that it would, but at the same time you can't help but fear the critics. Or you worry that people might not get it, or question what on earth is going on, or wonder if this weird guy might be exploiting his dogs. But more than that there was a nervousness that it *would* be popular, because of all that that would bring.

But by now I had spent too long thinking about the idea and getting it together to leave it unseen in the depths of my laptop. So what the hell . . . set it free and see what happens. And I told myself that I would be prepared for anything which might or might not follow.

But I never was. Once more it exploded and the same ride began on the viral video rollercoaster. In came the love, swiftly followed by the arrival of people offering a multitude of things, such as putting out a few Instagram posts with Olive and Mabel accompanying their product, or those who offered to run a subscription-only website based on my dogs ('The financial rewards could be SIGNIFICANT'). Essentially lots of people just spotting an opportunity – getting wind of something taking off and trying to grab on to the coat-tails, or dog-tails, of whatever it might be.

The other aspect of it was far more heartening. A colleague told me that his partner had been having a dreadful time at work and he sent me a video (with her permission, I should add), secretly filmed, of her watching the clip after coming home, squeals of laughter filling the house.

There is also undeniable fun and a sense of pride in watching it all unfold. Relatives in the Netherlands sent a clip of a TV panel show introducing highlights from all the videos with subtitles. 'Mabel with the heavy tail use' came my voice on the breakfast-eating clip as 'Mabel kwispelt hevig' appeared at the bottom of the screen. An approach came in from one of the major TV channels in Germany to appear on their breakfast programme called 'Frühstücksfernsehen' which, in a pleasingly literal Germanic way, translates as 'Breakfast Television'.

The performances of Olive and Mabel were bypassing language barriers and traversing the globe. An email arrived from Nippon

TV asking if they could show the videos on their national news programme. Naturally I said yes – as I loved the idea of Japan somehow taking to the story, or perhaps developing it further into a violent game show where contestants were licked into submission by giant Olives and Mabels as a host looked on, laughing continuously at their misfortune.

But again, the aftermath had something of a downside. For a start, it rather takes over your life and you simply struggle to get anything else done as you deal with the response. You try and shut it out, but it dominates your thoughts and Caroline and I both felt the strain of it. With neither of us having other work to distract us from the madness, it became all-encompassing.

There is a feeling that you are careering downhill and pumping away furiously at ineffective brakes. As well as the endless requests for interviews, there are also plenty of platforms on TV and online who would happily lift your content and use it for their own benefit without so much as a polite enquiry. There are others who do ask and if you say no, well, they just take it anyway. 'May we use your video? We'll give you full credit!!' became a very regular question on emails from all sorts of organisations. They might as well say, 'Could we use this thing that you have made and give you absolutely nothing!!' and no amount of exclamation marks or cheery demeanour is going to hide that. I was fast learning that it's very difficult to put out a video which takes off around the world and retain any feeling of being in control.

At one point I was contacted by somebody in India who had put my video up on his YouTube channel, where it had hundreds of thousands of views. He was claiming that I was infringing his right to make money from it. I read this email as I sat on the sofa with Mabel's head in my lap and had a little think about life. Then I discovered that my videos were filling the channels of several other users, all keen to cash in.

So, if it can all feel a little bit too much at times, then why do it? The honest answer is that I was trying to maintain and even build my profile, as a freelance broadcaster in days when not many people were requiring my lance. But it was also enjoyable – fun in trying to come up with the idea and execute it properly, gratifying to see it appreciated when it was released. It can be intoxicating – something which has more grounding in scientific fact than mere metaphor. When human beings complete a task or get some sort of approval, there is a tiny amount of a chemical called dopamine released into the brain. It offers an internal reward, which can cause an unwitting addiction.

Scanning the messages that were coming in (at a rate of about one every three seconds during the twenty-four hours following a video being put out), I was drowning in dopamine, getting dozens and dozens of little fixes, but the situation we were all in made it worse. With lockdown I was trapped in close proximity to an iPhone or laptop and, like a laboratory rat, I was just pawing away at the buttons which made me feel good. Or, rather more in keeping with the theme, I was the dog performing tricks for the reward of a biscuit. It probably wasn't the healthiest way to exist, but then none of what anybody was going through then was good for our mental equilibrium.

Usually there is a way out of scenarios like that – a release valve. More often than not for me it is a trip to the mountains, taking Olive and Mabel and getting away from it all. It's something which I've been doing with my dogs for a good few years and something which I wanted and needed more than ever during that time of lockdown. Thankfully that way out opened up eventually and we were able to move around again. In addition, the rest of our lives have slowly improved and as a small, but not insignificant side-issue, sport has begun to take place. Once more I even find myself commentating on actual humans, which I'm not saying I prefer, but it does pay the bills.

And, on that rather vulgar topic, a lot of people have asked if I made any money directly from success of the behemoth videos. To which the short answer is no, although clearly there have been spin-offs – for example, you are reading this book which you have either bought, stolen or borrowed (any of which I thank you for). Somebody did work out that the accumulated views of more than fifty million for the early videos would earn you about $200,000 in advertising revenue on a platform like YouTube, whereas on Twitter – nothing. And yes, that somebody was me. I did eventually get accepted for monetisation on YouTube, which is when they start to put advertisements for all manner of unnecessary products around your videos and then pay you a share of the revenue. But it was all too late to catch the big wave and, besides, I didn't really want it to be about that.

'Come on . . . I did it all for a love of my dogs and just wanting to make people laugh,' I say, as I grind my teeth down to the gums.

But one thing I have taken from a very strange period where we rolled up and down through peaks and troughs, is to try and be more positive – to see the fun in things where possible and to be more optimistic in difficult times. To be... how shall I put it? More . . . Labrador.

I can't guarantee that they are always the wisest or most well-researched counsel, but in terms of tackling life with a spring in the step and a sunny disposition we could all learn something from our dogs.

Goodness knows I've had plenty of teachers over the years.

6. The Dogs That Came Before

M y grandparents had thirteen dogs. Yes, I agree, that does seem rather excessive.

Shetland sheepdogs they were and the woolly flocks of those islands must have been living a life of carefree abandon, since practically every member of the breed appeared to be in my grandparents' house. The reason was that they had been chased out of Germany (my grandfather's native land) by the Russians, forced to abandon both home and livelihood. As a result, when they ended up in my grandmother's country of Scotland they turned their hands to several ventures. They kept a pig or two and I think the odd cow may also have been involved at some point in proceedings. For a spell they were turkey farmers, and then finally decided to try their hand at dog breeding. I'm told that they weren't particularly successful at it – although the sheer numbers would suggest that somebody was clearly doing something right.

By the time I came along there were only about five of the sheep-dogs remaining, but quite enough to be going on with and certainly sufficient to shape a child into feeling comfortable around our canine friends. While also convincing that same child that having an entire pack of dogs in your kitchen was perfectly normal.

My other grandparents had two West Highland terriers – whiskery old gentlemen who seemed to live in a permanent state of being cross about something. They also just kept on going as smaller dogs often do, becoming harder of hearing and a bit less sprightly, but generally pottering around until they finally departed at some indeterminate age, possibly their mid-thirties.

It's no surprise then that a good number of photos of our child-hood feature a dog – me and my two older brothers, Stephen and Colin, with a furry beast nearby. One of my favourites is of our own Shetland sheepdog, Kelpie, coveting a small cake held temptingly in my eighteen-month-old hand. But dogs were always there in roles of varying prominence – lurking in the background, busying themselves with some matter of great importance, or even just offering the edge of a nose poking into shot. Very occasionally they would be front and centre of the group, posing in noble fashion and appearing to be cooperating fully with proceedings but really being held there against their will with a firm hand, or bribed to stay in place with a subtly located biscuit.

We did have cats as well, but cats have a tendency to wander on to roads, so they came and went with more regularity. I think my mother tried to get successors with the same markings in the hope that I wouldn't ask too many questions requiring the deft reply that our former cat had 'just gone on holiday for a while'. Eventually we found one who knew to look both left and right and was with us for all of my childhood – Ludwig, named after the mad Bavarian king who spent much of the Crown wealth building castles. Although the greatest extravagance of our own Ludwig was the occasional dead mouse or bird left in a shoe.

I am fond of cats – I can safely say I have a soft spot for all animals. At the 2019 World Athletics Championships in Doha I bought some cat food for the scrawny kittens I had found living in the car park between the stadium and the enormous, air-chilled shopping mall. Every day I would take them a bowl of water and leave another pile of Kitty Chow, much to the bemusement of the locals. It was a grim place for any animal to grow up and I fear they have probably now gone the way of our early non-traffic-savvy felines, but I just wanted to give them a fighting chance.

The issue I have with cats is that they can be rather distant. And by rather distant I mean total bastards. They draw you in for affection with a purr or by coiling themselves around your legs, you then administer the soothing stroke or scratch behind the ear and, for some reason best known to themselves, they repay you with a full-on assault.

Dogs, by contrast, offer constant and easy love. You don't have to work too hard to get their unfettered adoration and no stroking, tickling or patting will go unappreciated. And that feeling of love is reciprocal – above all, I think, if you are exposed to dogs early on. Whenever I see a child on a walk who is cowering behind the legs of their parents as our dogs advance, I always try and introduce them to the charms of Olive and Mabel. Granted, this is often ruined by Olive clinically separating a biscuit from the child's hand and, on more than one occasion, replacement ice creams have had to be purchased with fulsome apologies. But I know that if a child doesn't get to experience dogs, then the chances are they're not going to be a massive fan when they're older.

So, I have been comfortable around dogs for my whole life. Whether this explains a corresponding lack of human social skills I'm not sure – perhaps I should have been introduced to more people on my own walks as a youngster – but this is certainly something which I've had to address. In my line of employment, the ability to network is a serious asset and if company executives or heads of major broadcasting corporations were dogs then I'd be fine, but in my experience this is rarely the case. Or, if I could only treat people as I do dogs, then I'd manage rather better. Although the last time I approached the CEO of a major sponsor and tickled him behind the ear while asking him if he was a good boy, it didn't end well.

Even now, after nearly three decades of adulthood have forced me to acquire certain abilities in human interaction, if I enter a room of strangers, rather than starting up a conversation and mingling as normal people would do, I gravitate instead to any available dog. It might be a dinner party or some social affair at a house, in which case it will be the family pet who is the unsuspecting target for my affections. At official functions it can be more tricky and there have been a few times where I have talked at length with a guide dog then wandered off before realising that I hadn't said much to the owner other than, 'Can I touch your dog?'

Stadiums and sporting events offer different opportunities. Every day of the fortnight at Wimbledon – if you get there early enough – you'll catch the police dogs going about their business.

The spaniels, Labradors or collies hunting for suspicious bags and potential explosive devices, all for the reward of a tennis ball. At airports I'm one of the few people who is delighted to have my suitcase thoroughly inspected by the sniffer dogs. 'Sir, please do not interfere with the operative,' I was once told at JFK, as I leaned in for a brief petting session at the baggage carousel. Sometimes I think that even if I fell on hard times and resorted to being a drug mule and was singled out by a beagle after arriving on a flight from Bogotá, I would still be momentarily cheered up and would enjoy tousling his fur and telling him he was a very good dog, before being taken away for my twenty-year stretch.

Anyway, it's strange given my fondness for larger-breed dogs now that the dogs of my infancy were invariably on the small side. Another Shetland sheepdog, Peerie, came along when I was four. Picking him up in the car, his long snout nosing out of the basket alongside me on the back seat, is one of my first clear memories. Then, my incessant whining for a dog of my very own eventually paid off with the arrival, on my eighth birthday, of a Yorkshire terrier called Humfrey.

7. Humfrey

Perhaps, in my demands for a dog, I should have been a touch more specific.

Although growing up surrounded by West Highlands and Shetland sheepdogs, I'm not sure I even realised that other sizes were available, so when we collected Humfrey I wasn't at all concerned that he might not be the largest, manliest companion. He firmly believed that he was. Indeed I can safely say that at no point in his life did Humfrey suffer from a crisis of confidence.

When you mention to people that your first dog was a Yorkshire

Terrier you know that they are picturing a tiny, frail creature with long hair and a bow, or other fashionable accoutrements. I can understand the mistake, because if you ever watch Crufts then the representatives of that breed will invariably be coiffured to within an inch of their lives with the desired size appearing to be that of some sort of rodent – ironic, given that they were originally bred to savage the rats of Bradford mills. But Yorkshire terriers bred for show bear no relation to Humfrey, a stallion-like version of the breed who was utterly fearless. He was the boss.

Another clarification to offer is that, yes, Humfrey was spelled with an 'f' rather than a 'ph', just in case you are about to fire off a stern letter to the publishers. Maverick that I am, and was, I insisted upon it.

That maverick nature extended to my method of owning a dog, whereby I left almost all walking of him to other people. It's very strange given how much I love to stride out with my dogs now, but the early and heartfelt promises I had made, that *of course* I would feed Humfrey and take him out every day, came up against a fairly impressive opponent in the distracted nature of a child and then the overwhelming laziness of a teenager. For much of his life I was that clichéd combination of the child who loves the idea of dogs, but doesn't necessarily love the practical requirements. I liked a dog to have fun with and pet and stroke and 'be my *very* best friend forever and ever', but only if I could be bothered. If Humfrey presented me with a lead in his mouth and a hopeful expression, I might well tell him to bugger off and speak to my brother Colin, because I was in the middle of a really good game of *Manic Miner* on our ZX Spectrum.

Having said that, I really did love Humfrey. This was confirmed when, while he was still very young, he contracted a disease whose name sends shudders through dog owners: parvo. It is a particularly unpleasant virus, which very often ends up in a dog's life being over just as it is getting underway. I clearly remember being distraught at the sight of him lying stricken in his bed and being given the blunt truth that he may well not make it. For two days my mother and grandmother took turns in administering teaspoons of water to what seemed (and was) a near-lifeless ball, and then very slowly the ball began to recover. Gradually there was movement – eventually the head would lift for the water and by the time a small snack was accepted we knew he would make it.

And, thereafter, the life that nearly wasn't his was action-packed. I may have refused to do the daily, mundane walks but I did turn up – like some glory-seeking actor in the big scenes – for the truly adventurous expeditions, of which there were many. Indeed, some photos from childhood show the first intertwining of two of my major loves – dogs and mountains. Perhaps mountain is an ambitious description for Loudon Hill in East Ayrshire, but it would have seemed like Annapurna to an eleven-week-old Humfrey. Then there is a photo at the top of Goatfell on the Isle of Arran, where we spent many a summer holiday, my exhausted mother flanked by our two hardy beasts, both fresh as a daisy having galloped up and down the near 3,000 feet the equivalent of half a dozen times. I'm sure they were also there on Ben Lomond – the most southerly of the Munros[1] and the first one I climbed, as it is for most people from the south-west of Scotland. Often, in the snapshots of those days, Humfrey is seen with a rather rakish 1980s fringe draped over one eye, like a canine Simon Le Bon. On other occasions he sports

1. A 'Munro' is the name given to a mountain in Scotland over 3,000 feet in height, or 914.4 metres in metric terms. It comes from Sir Hugh Munro, a founding member of the Scottish Mountaineering Club, who drew up the list in 1891. With occasional promotions and demotions over the years due to more precise measurements, the list now stands at 282 peaks.

a more brutalist style when my mother had obviously had enough and found some scissors, but both he and Peerie threw themselves into life and seemed to enjoy everything enormously.

And those lives were not short. Perhaps thanks to a combination of that healthy outdoor lifestyle and the tendency to longevity of smaller dogs, Peerie and Humfrey went on until the ripe old age of seventeen, carrying me through to my own adult life. During all the pains of growing up, the innocent enjoyment of being a child and the angst and frustration of teenage years, they were there. With any failure or success with exams, sport or the opposite sex, and the attendant mood swings, they were ready to soothe me by just being close at hand – soaking it all up and listening. Or, at the very least, managing to give that impression, which is all that was required.

They were also, inevitably, the first dogs to bring me that great sadness at the end. I knew that they had to leave eventually, but I didn't really know what it would feel like when they did. With childhood seeming to stretch out for an eternity, it was as if they had always been with us and perhaps always would be. Later in life, with the years passing more quickly, you realise that dogs are here only fleetingly in human terms. It is the cruel trick played on us that our companions in life trot alongside for only a short part of that longer journey.

When a dog departs you also quickly discover who are, or are not, dog people. Those who tell you they know exactly how you feel and it's clear that they do, because they have felt it themselves. Others might shrug or laugh as one colleague did, or offer an ill-advised joke as if pondering the demise of a goldfish. And you know you will never be able to fully describe to them the sadness you feel or the hole that your dogs have left.

I am not a religious person and, soothing though it might be to hear, I don't believe I will bump into them again in some celestial dog-walking area. That said, Peerie and Humfrey both do occasionally still feature in my dreams. Even as I sleep I do the calculations that they were born in 1977 and 1980, but I don't query this too much or wonder what their regimes might be to have them still hale and hearty heading into their forties. All I know is that I just feel a deep contentment as I doze. So perhaps we do occasionally see them again and, like all beloved dogs, they live on long after they have gone.

But still, it really was the end of something more when they went – Peerie while I was at university; Humfrey in the early days of my first job. With each one of them it felt like I was saying goodbye not just to them, but to a part of my life which had now closed. You know you are going to miss them. I think you know, too, that you will miss those days of the past as well.

However sad the ending, dogs were firmly, indelibly imprinted on my soul. My upbringing meant that I would always be one of those that they call 'a dog person'. It was just that another stage of life was about to get in the way and they would have to slip, if only for a while, into the background of the photograph.

8. Dogless Days

In the enormously budgeted film which is obviously going to be made of this book – should Ryan Reynolds ever return my calls – this is where we hit a montage. 'London Calling' by The Clash kicks in as the landmarks of the capital flit across the screen. It's the next phase, a new chapter is beginning and you're left in no doubt that we have moved on to one of the most exciting cities in the world.

Then there is the needle-scratch on the record and the comedy scene-wipe to the reality of an overnight shift at the BBC, reading sports bulletins and surviving on inadequate food from a vending machine. Yet even that was strangely exciting. Not the vending machines, I had seen them once before on a trip to Glasgow – but just to be at BBC Television Centre, where so many of the programmes I had watched growing up had been made. So much of the way I had seen the world had been shaped by this place and, in the small hours, I could wander through empty corridors and studios as if on a sightseeing tour. Look . . . here's the studio where they made *Top of the Pops*. Hey . . . that's where they tap-danced on *Record Breakers*! And the Blue Peter Garden just outside there . . . Is this the studio where they read the main evening news? It is. Ah, it's so *small* . . . And over there, that's the desk where a sports broadcaster eats a slightly stale sandwich at four a.m. tweaking a story about Arsenal's latest signing and thinking about what might be in years to come.

All those things, all those glimpses of a glamorous world (or at least that's how you think of it then) are tantalisingly close. You can see the destination, you just might not be able to work out exactly how you will get there. But still anything seems possible, because in your twenties the world is yours to be claimed and you have the energy and drive to do so.

What you haven't got is the urge to have a dog, as you're too busy with that grand plan of yours. There were a lot of things which I put aside after moving south. You become so immersed in the life you have chosen there and the career you are trying to build, that the job becomes all-important to the detriment of many things which you have previously held dear.

Besides, London is no place for a dog anyway – no big cities are really, but as much as the place was wrong, the time was more of a deal-breaker. Canine care is not compatible with the life of somebody working the long and irregular hours of the media. Added to that, I was a swinging young bachelor in one of the most happening cities in the world. Why wouldn't I be out partying hard and living life to the full as well? A question I asked myself many times as I sat watching television while eating a Pot Noodle.

I'm not sure what percentage of dog owners are in their twenties, but I'd guess that it's not high at all. Dogs are time-consuming and depend on us entirely. It's an investment that they fully deserve. Again, cats would be a slightly different matter, because of their relative self-sufficiency – give them a cat-flap and most will be fine, although a city address would demand even greater levels of knowledge of the Green Cross Code. You can also leave cats an enormous pile of food with the instructions that they should ration it out over a few days and they will. Do the same with the vast majority of dogs and before you can say 'now this is to last you until Tuesday' the pile will be gone and they'll then be asking if they might possibly have just a little bit more.

So dogs were most assuredly not part of proceedings as I started out at the BBC. That's not to say that there wasn't still one in my life – there was. It's just that I had visitation rights only once in a while when I made it back to Scotland. Because, before I moved down to London, our family had taken ownership of another hound. And substantially upgraded in size.

9. Suilven

It was entirely my fault. After the smaller dogs of my youth, in my late teenage years I had become smitten with the bullmastiffs belonging to a friend of my mother. Anybody who is familiar with those breeds will know them as the most gentle of souls. Yes, enormous and capable of eating their own vast bodyweight every five minutes if given the chance, but thoroughly loveable. So, a few years later, shortly after Humfrey had gone, when I was just starting my first job at Scot FM radio station in Edinburgh, my mother and I went to collect a puppy which was already larger than any full-grown Yorkshire terrier.

Suilven was beautiful – named after the famous and striking mountain of Assynt in the far north-west of Scotland and not dissimilar in scale. She was totally amoral and all the more wonderful for it, clearly meaning no harm, but if her heart was set on something she would just take it. Utterly immovable mentally and often physically.

Suilven wasn't alone. My mother had also taken in a couple of rescue dogs, Ben and Katie. They appeared to be part-collie, part-lurcher, part-Alsatian, part miscellaneous, but it was never that clear as to their exact provenance and we thought it rude to ask.

The sentiment of taking in rescue dogs is noble and the act is very necessary, but it does mean that those dogs often come with certain issues. They are, after all, dogs who may well have had a wretched start in life, needing to be re-homed after being abandoned or ill-treated. Ben was consequently the most nervous of fellows and aeroplanes, in particular, were far beyond his comprehension. If one appeared in the sky while out on a walk – which wasn't unheard of under the flightpath of Prestwick Airport – he would simply bolt for home, and be found later on beneath a bush in the garden. But, with the minor frustrations of dealing with his angst, there was enormous satisfaction that a dog who had a grim start in the world was now being given the best life possible.

Katie really belonged to my brother Colin since he did all of her walking – or sprinting, as she had decided that the sole meaning of her existence was to chase down tennis balls. And who could blame her? She had been saved from a life which involved being cooped up in a caravan for much of the day. Now, with the beach on her doorstep, she was going to enjoy every moment, even if that meant running herself into a slightly staggering dizziness.

All this meant that when returning from London I couldn't help noticing that our old family home was now approaching the levels of my grandmother's kennel-like abode. But Suilven was the star – and one around which we all fell into orbit.

What did she do to earn this status and affection? Absolutely nothing. That really is part of the charm of bullmastiffs. They don't have many tricks or an ability to turn on the standard dog cutesie-ness – they just wander round in a world of wanting things.

I think my attraction to bullmastiffs is in the size as well. There's a bit of the bovine in them and something about the large, perhaps a bit clumsy and – dare one say it – slightly less cerebral creature that appeals. Whereas with a Border collie you can see the brain working away behind sharp eyes, with bullmastiffs there is little going on but the occasional blink.

Yet if there is something that they desire, then their focus and commitment to getting it is extraordinary. On my trips back north I would always make sure that Suilven slept beside my bed in my old room. She had her own cavernous bed on the floor, containing her own duvet, but in the middle of the night she would usually decide that my small single bed and duvet was a more attractive prospect. So in the dark the questions would start to be asked – a low whine then a couple of snorts. You knew this was the build-up to a full-on mastiff *woof* which, if you haven't heard it, is quite something – if cows could bark it would be similar – and before it arrived and woke up the household and piqued the interest of various seismologists, I would have to extend an invitation to join me.

But this was far from the end – it only signalled the beginning of a rather laboured procedure. Mastiffs do not include grace and elegance in their skillset, so I would hear noises that suggested great effort for a few minutes, the huffing and straining eventually forcing me to switch on the light to see that, after all that, only her front paws have reached bed level and she is staring at me with the still blank expression, but one which now contains just the faintest trace of 'I would appreciate your assistance in this matter'.

And so I do assist and she thanks me in her own way, taking her place in the middle of the bed before I can get back into position. Within moments she is producing that special mastiff snore that comes from a combination of enormous bulk and a squashed face and I am shivering, having decisively lost the duvet battle with eight and a half stone of dog.

But, even though I was sleep-deprived, I loved my trips back home and at the end of every flying visit it was hard to say goodbye and return to the very different world of London. Leaving Suilven with her ungainliness, bed-theft and uncomprehending stare was always the most difficult part of all, even if she were only wondering how this might, in any way, affect her.

10. Escape to the Country

There was certainly an element of homesickness in the early
days down south – one of the symptoms of which was a
rekindling of my love for the mountains. Living in Scotland I had
begun to take them for granted. As is often the way when you have
something close by – if not on your doorstep then certainly within
a couple of hours – you might not make use of it quite as much
as others do. Like people who live just a few blocks away from the
Sistine Chapel and consider it just that place with the fancy ceiling
on the way to the shops. But, in London, the mountains became

something of a distant ideal. They were an obvious contrast to that cluttered and busy life – once again, it was the notion of escape. And the desire to be there more often was also sparked by a particular trip back to the country I still considered home.

Friends from university days decided that we should hold a reunion each spring. The plan was that the four of us would enjoy a weekend in Glasgow, revisiting old haunts and throwing in a hill walk for good measure, with the selection of the particular hill left to me. We didn't want to venture too far, because it was more about being in the city where we had shared four great years, earning largely pointless qualifications and memories which have proved far less redundant.

Now, for most people who live in or around Glasgow, there are two mountains which appeal. There is the aforementioned Ben Lomond, sitting on the north-eastern edge of the famous loch. Or, a bit further to the west but only forty-five minutes from the city, the Cobbler. Just short of the 3,000 feet required to qualify as a Munro, but far more interesting than many bigger beasts, it would be our peak for the day.

I had known its name and reputation for many years. My father was a keen hillwalker and 'Off to climb the Cobbler' was a well-known phrase when we were staying in my grandmother's house in nearby Kilcreggan. Now, of course, I realise that he probably just had to get away from the dogs. The actual name of the mountain[2] is Ben Arthur, but this is only for maps of a certain vintage – everybody knows it as the Cobbler, as the outline when you approach

---

2. The difference between a 'hill' and a 'mountain' is often debated, but there is no precise answer and certainly no exact height at which one becomes another. A mountain does suggest something bigger and perhaps more pointy in its shape, but in Scotland the two words are almost interchangeable and that's how they'll be used in this book.

from the east is supposed to look like a shoemaker working away, bent over his last.

Part of that outline is the reason it is such an exciting peak, with the central summit rising in a column that takes some nerve to scale. You crawl through a small window in the rock – known as Argyll's Eyeglass – and find yourself on a sloping ledge, then creep round, as close to the pillar as you can, with a fifty-foot drop by your side, and clamber up on to the top. Legend has it that every chief of the Clan Campbell, historically the dominant clan of these parts, had to prove his manhood by performing the manoeuvre.

There are plenty of hillwalkers who have never made it to the top in years of trying, but the good news was that we all proved sufficiently manly and, when returning to London, I was able to take my rightful place as the chief of my household of one. But the climb had been exhilarating, the weekend a major success and the legacy was that I was utterly hooked on the hills again.

In the weeks, months and years to come, I would head for the pointy bits of the country whenever I could and threw myself in at the deeper, or higher, end of things. That final summit block on the Cobbler had given me a taste for scrambling (the activity between hillwalking and full-on climbing, where hands are necessary and some people even like the safety of a rope). Aonach Eagach in Glen Coe was quickly followed by the nearby Curved Ridge on Buachaille Etive Mòr and Tower Ridge up the northern face of Ben Nevis produced a never-to-be-forgotten outing. In hindsight it was wise that I was getting these routes done in my dogless days, as even the most talented and agile of them struggle with handholds. There were some simpler mountains conquered along the way, but there was never any question of taking Suilven with me. Bullmastiffs and gravity do not get along and she would frankly be insulted that I had asked.

Meanwhile London life continued and I met Caroline, who also worked at the BBC. Of course, key to the early stages of any relationship is finding out what common tastes and interests you have. Some compromise was reached on mountains – we did both climb the aforementioned Suilven, but it has never been a shared passion. Caroline is very keen on long walks, but I also require that a steep gradient be involved and if I don't end up a couple of thousand feet higher at some point then I feel somehow let down. On one subject, though, no humouring or feigning agreement was required, because it quickly became apparent that we both loved dogs.

Caroline had grown up in a household with flat-coated retrievers – longer-haired cousins of Labradors and equally happy souls. So, while dogs were not front and centre, they were always there as a subplot to our London story. 'We will get a dog,' was an almost unspoken acceptance. Or, we would talk about it more openly, even mulling over the possibility of a London dog. But it just wasn't practical – both of us still working flat out and travelling a great deal.

Instead, we lived vicariously as dog owners. We made regular excursions to Richmond Park – the vast former hunting ground of Charles I which, even in a city, can make you feel just briefly that you are in the countryside. And every one of these walks was filled with games of dog bingo. How many breeds can you spot? Or asking strangers, 'Do you mind if I say hello to your dog?' and those strangers beginning to look uncomfortable when you're still there, ruffling ears twenty-five minutes later with even the dog now saying, 'Look, we really should be leaving now. This is getting weird.'

I even briefly considered moonlighting as a professional dog walker, as it seemed to be a thriving business in the parks of London. As far as I could make out, the necessary qualifications were an ability to squash a dozen or more dogs of varying sizes and temperaments into a Ford Ka with 'Walkies While U Work!' written on the side. This probably advertised better than the truth, which would be 'Zero control of your dog, but it's twenty quid a head!'.

Instead, we just did what we could to get our dog fixes. There was once a trip to see a friend's aunt, who was a breeder of Labradors, with the freely-admitted intention of rolling around on the ground among the puppies. At one stage there was a contest to see how many I could cover myself in – and such was the company that nobody raised an eyebrow. In fact I think I briefly had dogs for eyebrows and managed eight in total, before two who had fallen asleep on my chest, slipped off.

And of course I had my semi-regular trips back to Ayrshire where the canine Suilven, now in stately middle-age, would acknowledge my return with a brief wag of recognition. Then returned to her more pressing task of forcing somebody out of the chair that she had set her sights upon, by making a noise similar to a cow in distress.

If we had felt that we were going to be in London forever then things would have been different. Obviously, for millions of people, London is their home for good – those who are not just passing through in the formative years of a career. Among them are plenty of dog people, who have to add one to their household and just make use of the parks or settle for walks down the pavement. It's a poor substitute for beaches or fields or mountains, but dogs don't think about what they might be missing or worry about what they don't have. They simply enjoy what's on offer and if we'd been forced to stay it's the only option we would have had too. Fortunately, a way out was about to reveal itself.

One of the certainties of life is that it keeps moving on and, with every passing year, seems to accelerate as well. I remember sobbing away in our flat when the phone rang with the news that, as is often the case with bigger dogs, Suilven had gone at the very tender age of nine. You can't help but ask yourself, 'Where did that go?' Even when dogs have been more of a subplot, they can affect you enormously. I think I cried as well because she was supposed to be my dog and I was not there with her. In all honesty I had been elsewhere for most of her life.

Shortly after Suilven went came the news that BBC Sport was going to be moving their operation from Shepherd's Bush in West London to Salford Quays in Greater Manchester. And while many employees seemed to view this as something approaching the end of days, for me it brought a feeling of enormous relief.

There's no doubt that parts of my dozen or so years in London were wonderful – chances taken, experiences had, the world opening up. I had fun and achieved goals and met people and travelled far and wide. It was all the things, good and bad, that you would expect – twelve years of some very exciting times in my career and life, which I'm rather glossing over here. Perhaps they will one day be chronicled in a book entitled *Some very exciting times in my career and life*.

But London was never really for me. A city will suffocate certain people and one that size even more so. All you feel is the noise and the stress, when all you want is the quiet and the space. It was just a necessity that had to be endured for the job and now the job was moving. Well, Caroline's job really – she was based in the BBC office while I was all about events and could have been living anywhere close enough to an airport. So we headed north.

From a selfish point of view I would have been delighted, but it was a move which both of us wanted. Caroline's family are from the north-west of England and would now be near enough at hand. It also meant that I was closer to the mountains – certainly within striking distance of the Lake District or North Wales, still a long way from the great Scottish peaks, but regular trips were made there and now in half the time.

Our life in general was suddenly very different. Even living not too far from the major centres of Liverpool and Manchester, the pace had slowed when compared to London. You can feel the background noise lowering and the space opening up. There is now a garden and there is countryside on the doorstep. It seems that there is perhaps just one thing missing to complete a family.

It was time to get a dog.

11. Decisions

'Cocker Spaniel?'
For a few months before we became dog owners this was a familiar enough sound in our house – no other words required to form an actual sentence, just a dog breed uttered with a questioning intonation. And the debate would begin.

The problem is there are just too many to choose from. No other creature on earth has the same range as dogs, although I really haven't done any scientific investigation into this, so please don't contact me if it's not true. But if you were to present an alien invader with a chihuahua and a Great Dane and insist that yes, these were absolutely from the same genus, you would likely be blasted into atoms for your deceit, while the two dogs would ask if the newcomers possibly had any food. Cats would already have switched sides.

My point is, the variety of dogs on offer is extraordinary.

Every one of them man-made as well. Okay, the dogs have played a significant part, but centuries of selective breeding have created all the different types we know. Yes, you can go outside the confines of the Kennel Club lists and find dogs whose parents have done their own selecting, but if you choose a recognised breed then you are getting a dog that somebody at some point has decided was necessary.

We humans have played Dog God, shaping and creating them to make our lives better – originally for work, then for companionship and sometimes now for our own convenience. Every breed has a reason for being brought into existence.

Sheepdogs, gundogs, guard dogs and any number of terriers as pest control agents. Even bullmastiffs, whose CVs now read 'eating machine and sofa-stealers', originally had gainful employment, bred to be gamekeepers' dogs, specialising in capturing poachers and holding them down without doing serious harm – it's the innate kindness of the breed that they at least wait for fair trial. Yet sometimes it doesn't sit too comfortably that we get out our genetic dog modelling clay and sculpt something to suit our own purposes, without necessarily considering the health issues. For example, Dachshunds – literally 'badger dogs' in German – were created to flush out those creatures and even though many of them now have spine problems, I'm not sure if the future welfare of the breed was ever raised at any design meetings:

'Thanks for coming everyone. I'm sure you've noticed the serious issue with the badgers in the surrounding fields at the moment, but the obvious problem we have is that our dogs are all normal sized. Well, what if – and bear with me on this one – we were to fashion a dog with the head and body of a standard hound, a really quite aggressive temperament but also the legs of a sturdy gerbil? All those in favour . . .'

You'll have recognised that all of the jobs for which these dogs were designed are fairly ancient lines of work (and more often than not involved the demise of other creatures). With changing times they have adapted as we all have and become the aforementioned sniffer dogs – seeking out explosives or narcotics – assistance dogs, or even turning those noses to detecting certain illnesses. It can only be a matter of time before we are breeding dogs specifically for other modern lines of employment. Dogs designed to be social media influencers, with the in-built patience to sit still for any number of selfies or filming. I may have already made a significant contribution to this stage of dog evolution.

But when choosing a dog, how do you select from the enormous catalogue we have created?

For some the choice is partly dictated for them – they may not have too much space, so a smaller dog is required. They may be older owners or not be able to exercise that much, in which case you seek out a breed from the more lethargic end of the scale.

They may have allergies to shedding fur in which case, hey, we can accommodate you as well with dogs like poodles, shih-tzus or Tibetan terriers. Or, they may have small children, in which case a terrier who shares the floor with another small, occasionally yelping creature, may not be the wisest move.

When we were coming to make our choice we had few restrictions and our own dog-owning history had covered all creatures great and small. But there were still a couple of boxes which had to be ticked. Neither of us was particularly drawn to the more petite end of the market and certainly not toy dogs – the ones invariably described as having 'great characters', which often means they're just quite angry and ready to vent that anger on whoever might be nearby. The new member of our club also had to be up for serious exercise.

Walking for hours? Check. Running? Yup. Climbing a mountain? Absolutely.

And so the field narrowed.

As mentioned, a working cocker spaniel was briefly considered – the exercise and the mountaineering would be well within its scope. I was concerned, though, about the personality of the breed, which could best be described as 'highly motivated'. Every time I had met one on a walk it seemed to be in a permanent state of mania – tongue lolling, tail a blur, eyes wide as if five espressos into the day. To try and communicate with them, or open any kind of dialogue seemed pointless. I couldn't fault them for energy or effort, I would just like it dialled down a fraction.

We also talked about the possibility of a beagle, handsome inquisitive hounds that they are. Then, reading the small print, we discovered that they had more than a passing interest in wandering off. From many testimonies on the breed it appeared that if you were to unclip one only momentarily from a lead, the chances are that the next you would hear from it would be a few weeks later when a well-chewed postcard arrived from Turkmenistan. And indeed, every time I have subsequently come across a beagle on a walk it has been well shackled – owner at one end of the lead looking a little bit stressed and dog on the other, pretending to sniff around, but in reality plotting its escape.

And so, when we considered all the factors we kept coming back to one name – Labrador. Yes, I can hear some of you stifling a yawn now. Could you not be more original? Did you not want to try something different from the world's most popular breed? Well, no – there is a reason that they have that title. They are just outstanding dogs.

Other breeds drift in and out of fashion. French bulldogs seem to have been riding a wave for a while (mental note – idea for next video) and Huskies appear to be popular in many entirely inappropriate climates. Then there are those dachshunds which are cute, don't take too much exercise and have been photographed in the clutches of a couple of celebrities. As a result they are currently to be seen everywhere, flying along at their top-end speed and wondering how on earth people are managing to pass them at a brisk stroll.

Labradors don't fall in or out of favour. They let the other dogs have their day, living by the canine equivalent of the sporting credo that 'form is temporary, class is permanent'. They just carry on being near-perfect – relentlessly optimistic and friendly, good tempered and handsome. Slightly greedy, that's all.

One of the criteria which I also needed to have satisfied was that our dog had to be eminently strokeable. What is the point of having a dog if you don't want to caress its head or ears at regular intervals? Hypoallergenic fur is all well and good, but the tight and springy curls of a poodle just don't cut it. A Labrador is a velvet cushion in animal form – short coat, perfect domed head and ears made from the softest material known to man, woman or beast. As if created for therapy and designed for the purpose of stroking. Indeed, I believe the very first of these dogs on record was bred in 1782 by Spanish nobleman, Don Alvaro de Labrador, who wanted '. . . a beast simple and loyal, with coat of silke on which to rest my hand and ease wearisome mind' (*On the Origins of Dogs* by Andrew Cotter – don't look, I think it's out of print).

Apart from the tactile benefits, we knew that if we got the right type of Labrador, a slimmer one from working lines, as opposed to those bred for show which tend to be on the chunkier side of things, practically no outdoor pursuits would be off limits.

So the decision was made and now we just had to track one down.

12. Elsie – The Dog Who Never Was

You want a dog? If you're not going the rescue dog route, then . . .

First piece of advice – find yourself a breeder of some repute. If dogs are going on the cheap then there might well be a reason for this. If you are buying a dog from the newspaper ads, or from a bloke you were chatting to in the pub who has a friend who knows somebody with puppies, it might not be the best idea. You may not even be getting what was promised. Thought you were buying a pure-bred vizsla? Well, maybe the ears, the rest we can best put down as 'assorted'. Choosing a pedigree dachshund? No, that's just a mongrel kneeling down.

More seriously, and sadly, puppy-farming is a big and disreputable business. Run by those who are in it for the cold hard cash and won't have too many worries about genetics or care for the animals involved.

Instead we went straight to the Kennel Club website, found a list of Labrador breeders with healthy reviews and started phoning around. It so happened that the first one to get back in touch was in Devon. Not a problem – you can look locally for a breeder, but don't restrict yourselves. If you are getting a dog that is going to be with you for fifteen years or so at a good innings, then why would you not shop around a bit? A journey of a few hundred miles to find the right one is nothing in that grand scheme.

Then, a little bit of back and forth takes place – the best breeders will be assessing you as an owner as much as you are looking into them and I can only imagine the truth-embellishment which can occur at this point. 'Yes, we have many acres of land and of *course* we are very experienced dog owners. Now, what kind of batteries do they use?'

We were also asking our own questions – above all keen to find a puppy with a perfect hip-score. As I mentioned, Labradors have very few failings, but there can be a tendency to a suspect hip or elbow. Fortunately both the parents of the latest litter available, father Henry and the more exotically named mother, Bisto, fared well in that respect. So with breeder and potential owner satisfied, agreement was reached and the decision was made. We would collect Olive in a few weeks' time.

Although of course at that time she wasn't Olive – she wasn't anything. A dog with no name. I'm ignoring her Kennel Club title, which is the best thing for it. These are the lines of gibberish which are inflicted upon dogs at their official registration, as if breeders are forced to take vast quantities of opioids before filling in the form. You may have heard them at Crufts as the dogs enter the parade ring.

'Here comes Jinty – or 'Glory of the Dawn Over a Milton Keynes Roundabout' to give her full name. Lovely stride . . .'

But finding the right name can be tricky and don't go for one simply because it seems mildly amusing at the time. Imagine yourself shouting it on a beach, possibly in anger as said dog refuses all commands and heads for the dead seagull. Long before Olive and Mabel went viral you may remember the owner of 'Fenton' desperately trying to halt him as he chased a herd of deer in Richmond Park. Imagine how much greater the man's suffering would have been if the fifty million views worldwide had been of him yelling 'Sir Barksalot' at the top of his voice. Although it might well have achieved an even greater number of views.

We had a few guidelines in place. Two syllables works best for the rhythm and I'm also quite a fan of dogs with more traditionally human names. I remember once meeting a small gang of Norfolk terriers who were introduced as Steve, Michael and David. We decided that we would also go for the kind of names that once were bestowed upon humans but now seem to exist only among the more elderly ranks of the Women's Institute. Think Maude, Agatha, Betty or Doris. And in the end we settled on Elsie.

But, of course, it's a big decision, as that name is for life. For example, my own name was originally going to be Mungo, after the patron saint of Glasgow, but thankfully my parents eventually saw sense, and perhaps also a future of any number of fairly intense school beatings, and opted for something more conventional. On a side note, eight months before we got Olive my mother had taken ownership of a new bullmastiff puppy and called him Mungo. She was clearly just determined to call something, anything, Mungo.

But get the wrong owner and a poor dog may be in trouble. Once in Totnes, the old hippy hangout on the south coast of Devon, we were at a café and spotted a couple of dogs beneath the next table.

'What are they called?' I asked as I scratched the nearest ear.

'That's Shirley Temple and this one is Cat Stevens,' said their owner.

'Well, hello there, Shirley . . .' I said, continuing to scratch.

'No . . . not Shirley . . . Shirley TEMPLE,' came the firm reply.

Chastened, I tried to mutter something appreciative but I caught the eye of Cat Stevens, who I was sure looked a little bit ashamed. And I imagined his days in the old schoolyard and how difficult they must have been.

Anyway, by the time we went to collect our own 1970s singer-songwriter, we had changed our minds – a fact which we only revealed to Helen, the breeder, a couple of days before, so that her diligent weeks of calling the puppy Elsie, to try and get it to seep into her formative puppy brain, were all pointless. But we were resolute. Small and black, we had settled on another name. Elsie was no more. This dog of ours would be called Olive.

13. Puppy Love

Whatever her name as a puppy, Briefly-Elsie-Now-Olive was pretty much perfect. On the five-hour drive up from Devon there was scarcely a whine or a whimper. She was in a box with a blanket in the footwell of the car, either busying herself with a toy duck, or dozing at great length, or occasionally requesting that she might be upgraded to our lap. But never was there any sign of anxiety that she had been wrenched from her litter. It was just a case of, 'Is this what we're doing now? Fine. These people seem pleasant.'

I always marvel at how well she took to it. Being alone in the dark at night when up until that point all sleep had been against, or on, or under other warm dog bodies. But again that detachment from her siblings seemed to be taken in her short, slightly comedic stride. We did our bit to help as well – leaving her with a hot water bottle wrapped in a rug which we had taken down to her kennels to get covered in a familiar scent.

In fact, we were the ones who found it harder to get used to the change. In the pre-Olive years we had been used to sleeping in occasionally – now, for a child-free couple this was a glimpse of what that seismic change must be like. The difference with dogs is that the relentless-care phase does not last as long.

One thing that helps with puppies is that you can put them in crates, whereas with children I'm led to believe that is very much frowned upon. In all honesty, the puppies don't see the incarceration as any great hardship – in fact they come to think of the cage as their sanctuary. You leave the door open during the day and they will happily take themselves in there for an escape – a bit of me-time. Then, last thing in the evening, you cover it with a blanket as if trying to fool a budgie into thinking night has fallen.

Once more, Olive accepted all of this quite happily. I say all of it, but there was one solitary morning where we magically removed the cover of night to discover that she had soiled her bed. What you might not know is that in these situations puppies will try and remedy the situation by eating the incriminating evidence. Not so much for that reason, but for the fact they don't like to sleep in their own mess – and who does? But faced with the choice, you might think that just kicking it to the other end of the bed would be the lesser of the two evils.

So there's another point where puppies and children differ – as is the fact that children don't tend to eat their way through furniture. At least, not often. I had heard all manner of horror stories involving Labradors and their fondness for table legs, chairs, plants, cushions – in effect, anything made of atoms. Various fixtures and fittings would be shaved down in the early days by razor-sharp puppy teeth, then as the dog grows, chewed into pieces by sheer brute force.

Thankfully Olive-damage was minimal. Yes, toys had a life-expectancy measured in hours rather than years, but in terms of our own possessions she restricted it to the odd shoe and a short phase where her own beds were savaged in the middle of the night. I call this 'the absurdly expensive phase'.

I joke – the absurdly expensive phase of dog ownership is the whole thing. Insurance, food, toys, beds, more food, more toys, injections. And did I mention food?

Perhaps realising that my bank account was also being chewed through, Olive generously delayed the necessity of her operation to be spayed by being what the vet called, in less than medical terms, 'a bit immature in that department'. Eventually, at about eighteen months she did get her act together and in she went for the operation.

It might seem harsh, but it is often for the best with bitches. Unless you are intending to breed from them, or really want the attention of males from the neighbourhood and beyond, who would present their credentials, hair neatly parted, sporting a bow-tie and carrying a box of expensive dog treats. The good news was that when Olive came into season, she told every one of them to take their treats and their attentions elsewhere (actually, you can leave the treats). Often she did so with a quite dismissive, superior growl, as if laughing in their face, 'Um . . . I don't *think* so . . .' I did feel a sort of paternal pride at this, but at the same time recognised something of the dynamic and empathised greatly with the rather crestfallen suitor.

Still, even knowing that you have done the right thing, there is no sadder sight than a beloved post-op dog, still woozy from the anaesthetic, staggering towards you in the vet's surgery. Here she comes, whimpering and wagging a sorry tail, determined to give you the full greeting and delighted to see you even though you brought her here for this.

Actually, there is one sadder sight. And that is a dog in a head-cone. You know the ones, necessary to stop the dog from nibbling at any scar or stitches – so perfectly named 'The Cone of Shame' in the beautiful animated film *Up*. We did try all sorts of different types to make Olive's life easier. There was a softer cloth cone, which we quickly realised was useless, but also had the unfortunate side-effect of making her look like a canine Liberace. There was a giant inflatable disc which she wore like a Shakespearean ruff. It didn't work either and, if anything, only added to her embarrassment and sorrow at the whole affair.

It's just part of the early (yet immature in that department) stages of having a dog. Others would include a first swim, which I viewed with the pride that many parents might look upon the initial, faltering steps of a child. Pride, following just a moment of panic as it came about courtesy of Olive falling into the Bridgewater Canal. She thrashed around a bit until I hauled her out by the scruff of the neck and then sat for a good few moments staring at the water, wondering what in the world had just happened and how could she make it happen again.

And that's the thing about dogs. Their lives are run by a simple internal engine of wants and needs – driven purely by their desires, it's up to us to try and somehow control them, or at least rein them in a bit. How do we do it? Well, by cunningly using their own desires against them.

That, at least, is the theory.

14. Educating Olive

Dogs love to be trained, or at least to play a game that challenges whatever brain cells they might possess.

They are very willing to learn, but the trouble is that they don't get bored with the process quite as quickly as we might. We had also been reliably informed that dogs – or certainly Labradors – are desperate to please their owners and that this can be used very effectively in training. But with my experience of Labs now, I believe there is a clear hierarchy in their heads of what is most important:

Food
Food
Food
Also food
Human approval

And I'm not even sure that human approval should be as high as number five. Quite quickly we realised that receiving our gratitude and being told that she was a very good girl came pretty low down the list of priorities and we ended up instead relying on Olive's overwhelming greed to do the training for us.

Here's a good trick if you have a Labrador. Actually, trick does it a disservice – it is a recognised training aid. When they are young, every time they are eating a meal you blow a whistle, short and sharp, over and over again throughout the whole dining experience. Perhaps Olive felt that I was like a one-note version of the guitarist in a hokey restaurant, who sidles up to the table just as you're enjoying your starter, but the results were devastatingly effective. Subsequently, any time on a walk where Olive's concentration drifted to some other matter or she wandered off, there was a solemn nod from me to Caroline and the nuclear option was taken. A few blasts on the whistle and she would lift her head from whatever she had been doing – eating grass, eating sticks, eating a child's apple and fingers – and come sprinting to us as if her life depended on it. All for a tiny morsel of training treat and because we had conditioned her brain like evil geniuses.

Yet this was a minor triumph in a battle of wills. Olive has long since won the war.

It's mostly our fault for training her in a rather half-hearted way, or abandoning it when we thought we had it cracked. Labradors are some of the most trainable dogs you will find, but you still have to work at it. We only did a bit and as a result, Olive will obey us, but only when she decides that it's in her own interests.

We finally signed the treaty of surrender when, after two years of existing beneath us, staying in her bed or on the floor, she very nonchalantly one evening hopped up alongside Caroline on the sofa with a look that said, 'This is happening – get used to it.' It was a moment of huge physical and metaphorical significance. She had risen to our level, brazenly suggesting that she was now equal to us in standing. The next move would be crucial and the absolutely correct thing to do was to briskly shoo her back down to the floor with a scolding word. It might sound unkind, but it had to be done if we were to maintain order, discipline, and whatever dwindling respect she had for us.

Instead, they both settled down to watch *Coronation Street*.

But I think now it is perhaps that wilfulness that I like most about Olive. I don't really want a dog which has been utterly conditioned by us, submissive and bent to our will by rigorous training. Yes, I would like her to come back a bit more promptly, or indeed at all, when I get frustrated with her grazing on a walk, but I wouldn't change it.

Perhaps I love her personality because it seems not a million miles from my own. She could certainly be considered cheerier, but she also has her moments of saying, 'I don't want to do that, so I'm not going to – life's too short.' And in her case she would have a stronger argument. The well-known phrase is that dogs look like their owners, but in our case it is more that we occasionally appear to have a similar outlook on life. I'm well aware that I may be reading a bit too much into it and seeing things only because I want to, but there is certainly a strong connection.

Within the first few months of collecting her, I had become totally besotted. Of course, I had loved all the dogs I had known before, but because Olive was completely our dog – our decision, our choice, from when she was a glint in Henry's eye, to returning home with her and living every moment of every growing phase, the bond was far greater.

There was, though, one growing phase still to complete. Again it varies from breed to breed, but to play it safe with still-forming joints, black Labradors shouldn't be taken on truly arduous walks until they are about eighteen months old. You build them up very slowly, as we did with Olive.

Since leaving her native Devon she had done plenty of things and seen some sights – walking, swimming, eating, walking a bit further and eating a bit more, leaving nothing un-sniffed or un-chewed within a few miles of our house.

But now she was ready and it was time to expand her horizons. It was time to head for the hills.

15. First Dog Climb (The Ascent . . .)

Dogs, like humans, have their frailties and failings. Some might be a bit short-tempered, others (most of them) greedy and then there are those who err on the side of laziness. Combine that last one with their total honesty – an inability to hide their feelings and the fact that they are driven simply by what they want at that moment – and you realise that taking a dog on a mountain expedition can be a risky business. Even if you have a lithe and energetic breed.

I had remembered reading a newspaper story about a group of hillwalkers who had set off for a very long day and included in their number was a fit young boxer called Jarvis. At some point in the latter stages of the adventure a light had switched off, deep in the mind of Jarvis, and he had said 'enough's enough', so simply laid down and refused to go any further. Eventually the deeply frustrated and embarrassed party felt they had no other choice but to call mountain rescue, who dropped everything and arrived to carry Jarvis, in rather regal style, back down to civilisation. No note is made of whether the mountain rescue team brought their own search dog, to shake his head at Jarvis and tell him he had brought shame on their species.

I was fairly sure that no such incident would occur with Olive but there was still some trepidation as we drove north. Not too far north as I wanted it to be done in a day-trip from Troon, where I had stopped in to see my mother and Mungo, six months older than Olive and now the size of a small car. The destination was a couple of peaks within the Black Mount, just south of Glen Coe, and it would also be a reasonably short walk-in from where we parked the car, so that the day shouldn't be overly taxing for a debutante mountaineer.

I enjoyed the idea of taking Olive into the Scottish landscape. Even though she has Devonian origins, Labradors have strong ties to Scotland since it was (and this bit is actually true) Scottish peers the Earl of Home and the Duke of Buccleuch who were early developers of the official breed. But more of that later.

Yes, I might be stretching the homecoming a bit, but there was still a feeling of a special shared experience as we drove, heading off for an adventure together. Olive had no idea, of course, snoozing Jarvis-like, in the comfort of the boot (of an estate car rather than a saloon, as I'm not Joe Pesci in *Goodfellas*). I pointed out the landmarks on the route, so familiar to anybody heading from the south of Scotland to the mountains of the west and she expressed her keen interest in my presentation by snoring loudly. Over the Erskine Bridge we went, where the River Clyde widens to a firth and up the side of Loch Lomond on the A82 with the head and shoulders of the Ben looking down on the water. This is where you officially enter the Highlands – I tried to explain it to Olive then as I will to you now. I only hope that you don't react in the same way, by standing up, yawning, circling twice and collapsing with an audible sigh.

As a geographical concern, the Scottish Highlands are defined on the southern edge by the Highland Boundary Fault – a line which runs diagonally across the country – look at a satellite map of Scotland and you can see the distinct line of differing terrain, cutting through the Isle of Arran in the south-west and travelling all the way to Stonehaven, just outside Aberdeen on the north-east coast.

The Fault was active about 450 million years ago, as part of the same mountain-building phase that created the Appalachians in the United States. With the odd exception up around the Moray Firth, anything to the north and west of the fault-line is therefore, geologically at least, in the Highlands. South and east of it lies the rather busier Central or Midland Valley, where you find the major cities of Glasgow and Edinburgh – more often called the Central Belt in Scotland, because it is like a belt of lower land between the Highlands and the Southern Uplands.

In terms of land area, the Highlands and Islands occupy about half of the country, but in terms of inhabitants a far smaller fraction. That number is currently on the increase, but it is still one of the least densely populated areas in the whole of Europe. I knew Olive wasn't listening and I suspect that by now you might not be either, but I just feel that it is helpful information.

Anyway, we drove on into the Highlands, past Loch Lomond and through Crianlarich, overshadowed by the massive bulk of Ben More – the top half white with snow. Further on there was a glimpse to the left of Ben Lui, one of the most beautiful peaks, with twin ridges framing an enormous central face. Then through Tyndrum where the road forks left to head to Oban and the coast, or turns sharply right – as we did – and climbs, running by the railway line and the trail of the West Highland Way until you see the huge pyramid of Beinn Dorain. Soon we made it to Bridge of Orchy, turned down a single-track road winding its way to the end of Loch Tulla and reached our starting point. Olive slept through it all.

As well as my brief geography lecture, I realise that a language lesson may also be necessary, since I am already throwing some Gaelic names at you which may seem rather hard to grasp. Fear not, they do to most Scots as well. As a lowland Scot, any of the minimal Gaelic I speak tends to come from my time in the mountains. So here's a quick guide, keeping it as simple as possible.

Ben (or Beinn), Stob, Sgurr or Carn all mean variations of hill, mountain or peak, after which you might find an adjective to describe that peak, i.e. mòr, meaning big, dearg – red, ban – white. So, for example, Ben More (of which there are a few in Scotland) is pretty much the Big Hill. Càrn Mòr Dearg is the Big Red Peak. Pronunciation is a considerably more complicated matter which will often have you wondering, 'You arrived at *that* from this collection of letters?' But if spoken properly the sound of Gaelic has a beauty to match the places attached to the names.

Our first target of the day would be Stob a' Choire Odhair, or the 'Peak of the Corrie of the Winds'. The naming of it didn't concern Olive (Olibh) as we set off, but what did matter to her was that this clearly had potential to be a very interesting walk. Trotting alongside the River Shira, hopping into the shallows every now and again, spotting a stag on the other side and setting off, before realising it was all a lost cause – instead just giving it a firm stare, as if to say, 'I will spare you on this occasion, consider yourself fortunate.' It was all such an assault on her senses that she was already in high spirits before we turned into the climb itself and a short while later reached the moment which might bring the greatest joy in any dog's life – hitting snow for the first time.

It was an event captured on camera and remains to this day somewhere in the dark recesses of the internet on my YouTube channel. Yes, it's been dwarfed in viewing figures by other dog videos of the more recent past, but if you want to see what that climb was like and see Olive's ecstatic reaction to that snowy revelation, it is there.

When you look at a mountain in winter from a distance, you will see the snowline and it looks solid, as if it is just that – a line below which there is bare grass or rock and above it all is snow. Up close, it is a much more gradual transformation. First, tiny patches start to appear, the size of a footprint, then they get larger and eventually connect and you are into the world of white.

It was around about a thousand feet, somewhere between footprint-sized patches and complete cover, that Olive lost any control of mind and body. A step on to the snow, a micro-second for the feeling to travel from her paws to her brain and she was away. Whirling round and round like a dervish, leaping into the air and then running full speed on a loop of about five hundred yards, all because of this new sensation. 'Who knew the ground could feel like this! What strange magic is at play here?' Her unfettered joy was something to behold.

The novelty did wear off after a while, but it took some time. A thousand feet higher, with the snow getting deeper and having sunk in up to her chest a few times, it was rather more of an effort and she was perhaps regretting those five-hundred-yard laps. Then, as the temperature dropped, she began to ask more searching questions about the purpose of it all.

And that's when the bond tightened between us – that moment when you see they have put their total trust in you. 'This all seems a bit odd to me. Usually we're just once round the field and back, but the man seems to know what he's doing. So I'll follow him and stay close. Although...bear with... I might just briefly chase this snowball down the slope.'

Nearing the summit we stopped for snacks, which appeared to cheer Olive up considerably. 'If your dog is alert and still shows interest in food then they are fine,' was a bit of advice I had read. I'm not sure how accurate this is with Labradors, since they could have long since passed away, rigor mortis setting in, and still the nose would twitch if you waved a sausage in front of it. But a quick check with Olive and a bite to eat and she was clearly fine – just a bit confused by this strange environment.

Others, of the human kind, can also be a bit confused by the whole dog-in-the-snow thing. So, with regard to dog welfare, I think it's worth taking a moment here to put some minds at ease.

16. Paws Before the Summit

Throughout the entire Olive and Mabel phenomenon there has been almost no negative feedback on social media – and certainly nothing approaching Djokovic-fan levels of criticism. In fact, I can recall only one out of the tens of thousands of messages which expressed anything less than lovely thoughts. It came in from an account with a Donald Trump avatar (who knows, it may even have been the man himself) and this person suggested that the breakfast video was horrific as I had clearly starved my dogs for days beforehand to make them eat more quickly, all for entertainment.

I considered replying, to explain how he or she really didn't know the table manners of Labradors at all, but then thought better of it.

There were also a handful of other messages and emails which came in from those who had seen how much winter climbing I did with my dogs. These messages were not negative but suggested, in that well-meaning but quite forceful way of the internet, that I shouldn't be taking my dogs out in the snow without boots. One of the correspondents had even gone to the trouble of selecting the ideal set for me. Again, I didn't reply to too many emails during that time, but I was tempted with these ones, if only to tell them, in the most polite way possible, that this was nonsense.

Yet I could excuse the mistake. Before my own investigations I had even invested in boots for Olive – proper outdoor boots, meant for dogs working on ice, that cost more than most human shoes. There were just a couple of problems with this – the first major stumbling block being that dogs don't like wearing boots.

I had obtained a set from a very high-quality dog-outdoor-wear supplier and they did fit her paws well. But the process of getting them on took approximately seventeen hours. During this prolonged effort she stared at me with eyes that contained an impressive mixture of sadness for her own situation and contempt for me. Then, when cajoled to move she did so with the utmost reluctance, stepping gingerly about before beginning a quite complex dressage routine with a high-stepping gait as if trying to shake them off. Eventually she decided that the best thing to do would be to settle down and chew them into submission.

Secondly, and rather more importantly, you just don't need dog boots. Preparing thoroughly at the start of our mountain-climbing career together I made as many enquiries as I could – speaking to those who regularly took dogs into the hills. Mountain rescue were even phoned (I first had to explain that I was not in any danger, currently reclining on a sofa. And no, I had no idea who Jarvis was). I then headed for the internet which, if not always accurate, does contain information in abundance.

I wanted to know how it could be that dogs' paws don't suffer from frostbite as our feet surely would within a few minutes of treading naked through the snow, and I was directed to a study by a Professor Ninomiya from Yamazaki University, just outside Tokyo. Essentially, the report explained, dogs use the warmer blood from the heart to heat up the colder blood down at the paws, before returning it to the heart.

'Arterial blood flows to the end of their legs and then heats up venous blood before returning it to the heart,' said the good professor. 'They have a heat exchange system in their feet.'

Put more simply, dogs' paws don't get cold.

Not that they don't have any issues at all. The pads can get dry and cracked and it is possible to buy a type of dog-paw salve, but I have never even found that necessary. Indeed, you really don't want to soften them up – their pads are tough as old boots for the reason that they are a replacement for tough old boots.

There are other natural attributes which help out on winter days in the mountains. One being that Labradors have webbed feet. All dogs do to a certain extent, but some are far more webby than others and Labradors are at the frog-like end of the scale – it is one of the reasons they are such good swimmers. And on a wintry climb that webbing which they have between their toes acts as a sort of snowshoe, preventing the uncomfortable predicament suffered by many breeds, when snow turns to hardened balls on, and around, their paws.

Perhaps most importantly of all, Labradors have uber-efficient coats. Or rather, two coats. They have an undercoat which is soft and light, like a merino base-layer which we might pay a small fortune for, then there is the slightly rougher topcoat. The two layers combined work incredibly well at insulating, to the extent that I wouldn't feel the need to put an artificial coat on a healthy adult Lab until the temperature reached somewhere about minus ten or fifteen (for clarity, I'm operating in Celsius here, as I am not a monster).

Incidentally, that double-coat system is also a very effective waterproof, with oily secretions keeping water from reaching their skin. So don't wash your Labs too much as you'll dilute the protection. But those layers of fur also keep them cool in the summer, and insulate them from warm air. It never ceases to amaze me that Labradors can operate in a temperature range of fifty degrees Celsius wearing nothing but the fur they were born in. A five degree drop and we're looking for a thicker pair of socks.

That's not to say that Labradors are totally impervious to the elements. Later in our climbing career, Olive and I would be making a winter assault on Bynack More, in the heart of the Cairngorms when, on the ridge below the summit, the wind picked up as it so often can do in a mountain microclimate. Suddenly, a forty-mile-an-hour gale was howling in from the side with spindrift blasting us like gravel. Olive had turned entirely white on one flank, her ears flapping furiously and she made me aware, in no uncertain terms, that she was no longer enjoying the experience.

So, a mere eighty feet or so short of the top, we turned around. Knowing when to abandon a climb, even when so close to the summit, is one of the hardest, but most important calls an expedition leader has to be able to make. This expedition was small, but I still outranked Olive and she was very much in my care.

Of course, ten minutes into our retreat the wind had eased. The junior member of the expedition was happy – although requesting a constant supply of biscuits to assist her in dealing with the trauma – and I was left rueing the fact that we hadn't continued.

But that evening Olive couldn't settle – she kept trying to sit down and would then immediately bounce back up, nibbling at the base of her tail. As far as I'm aware, the entire course at dog medical school consists of licking, nibbling or gnawing – they are the only known cures for all ills, so I knew that something wasn't right. Back down south the next day and the vet, whose degree was more thorough, diagnosed 'dead tail' – more properly called Limber Tail and nothing too serious, just a bit of numbness that can occur in dogs who might have over-exerted themselves, or spent too long in cold water or extremely cold conditions. It would ease in a day or so.

It was a lesson learned and from then on I always kept a keen eye out for any signs of distress on winter climbs, while also administering frequent tail-base massages. And I would stress that from both Olive and Mabel they have always been gratefully received.

17. First Dog Climb
(Summit and Descent)

The conditions for that first climb on Stob a' Choire Odhair were chilly but certainly not extreme. So I was quite happy that Olive was fine, as we sat there snacking together – the only two creatures in sight and as close as we could be. I sipped tea from a flask and looked back down the mountain and saw two sets of prints in the snow, side by side – one made by two heavy boots and the other by four boot-less paws. Again, it was recorded for posterity and may not have the drama of many other photos taken

First contact. Olive.

And four years later . . .

Mabel happier with the new dynamic than Olive.

'I have all that I need.'

Mabel ready for her first walk. Without yet having mastered sitting properly.

Early expedition climbing the north face of me.

Dog and toupee combination.

The way of dogs: play hard . . .

. . . and recover.

Mabel lets her feelings be known on an early trip to Formby beach.

'I may not have told you in the last twenty seconds that I love you.'

Me and my brothers Stephen and Colin in our casual wear. Peerie pretending he's not with us.

Puppy Humfrey keen to escape from my polo-neck/shorts ensemble.

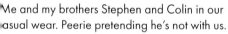

The enormous head of Mungo, losing the fight against gravity.

'Look what happened . . .'

The Liberace cone – fit only for comedy purposes. Which was enough.

'You say bath, but please first listen to my counter-argument.'

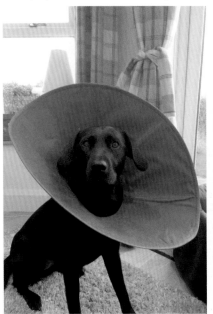

'The accusation is that I went into the peat bog, but where's your evidence?'

'I'm not so much angry with you, as disappointed.'

Olive and Mabel with the most respected member of our pack.

Mabel claims she is not a thief – despite all evidence to the contrary.

on mountain days, but it remains one of my favourites because of what that day was and what it meant. Our very first climb together.

A short distance further on, Olive now staying close to my side, and we reached the summit where the weather had closed in, and the views out over Rannoch Moor appeared only as brief, tantalising breaks in the cloud. With the wind starting to pick up and Olive's eyebrows gathering spindrift, she was beginning to look like a canine Denis Healey and I sensed that this might be enough for her, so we abandoned plans to go on to the more dramatic Stob Ghabhar and would save it for another day.

Besides, this adventure had been more than enough. The descent was quick and it wasn't long before we were crossing the bridge over the River Shira to the car – one of us carrying a sizeable stick as a memento, the other flooded with all the endorphins that an expedition like that could release. I briefly put down my treasured stick to get Olive's dinner out of the car and then, to round things off, she was served it al fresco with extra helpings and washed down by the cool clear waters of the Shira. I could see that she thought it had been a grand day for that alone.

It is difficult to explain just how joyous it was – how close I felt to Olive after that. It might sound silly, but if you are reading this book you are probably a dog owner and will certainly understand. The trust Olive had shown, in following me into a very strange environment without question (well, perhaps just a couple of gentle queries), the fun she had and all the new sensations experienced. It was everything I had wanted and as she hopped back into the boot to fall asleep within seconds, I removed damp, snowy gaiters and boots and couldn't stop smiling at the experience we had shared and what was now an even stronger connection between us. I'm sure she didn't give it quite the same depth of analysis or take from it all the emotions that I had, but I was certain she had enjoyed it.

The drive back down south would be tiring, but I already knew we would do this many, many more times. Not long into the journey and there were hearty snores coming from her enormous and well-furnished cabin – which I envied, as I began a fascinating lecture on glacial erosion in the Southern Uplands.

18. Mabel

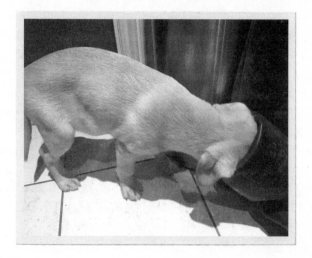

For four years Olive reigned in splendid isolation. The only child who wants for nothing and is probably a bit spoiled.

And one dog might be plenty. It might be more than enough, but there are things to consider when it comes to expanding the pack.

Firstly, there is just that – dogs are pack animals, historically used to wandering around in gangs, hunting or scavenging, scrawling graffiti about cats on underpasses, that sort of thing. And, as much as we might like them for companionship, they could also do with a bit of company of their own kind now and again. A fellow creature who may be more understanding when a nose is stuck into nether regions.

Also, on a rather more sensitive subject, there is a succession plan to consider.

Every dog owner tries to ignore, but is all too aware of, the fact that our dogs are likely to go before us. In which case the pain would almost be too much to be left with no dog for comfort in those times. And you should obviously try and space it out so that there are a few years between them – you don't want a dog to depart at fifteen and be left with an equally rickety thirteen-year-old. But don't leave it too long either – getting a puppy when your other dog is in its dotage means that neither of them will get the best out of the partnership, and the last thing an ancient dog needs is to be harassed by a deeply irritating puppy when it should be enjoying retirement in front of the fire. With the newcomer hanging from its ears, Dog the Elder would look up at you with eyes that say, 'Really? I give you all those years and you give me this clown? Also, don't think I don't know what's going on here . . .'

We felt that a four-year gap was about right, so that Olive and dog number two would be able to frolic and have adventures together for many a year. We also made a promise that it didn't mean there would be another puppy when Olive reached eight and one more at twelve – a new dog coming along every four years like the Olympics. That way madness lies, and possibly a house like my grandmother's.

Again, the next question to be answered was, what breed? We knew how good Labradors are, but should we try something different? Both of us had – and still have – a real soft spot for Staffordshire bull terriers. They are the most affectionate of dogs who simply require a decent PR company to salvage their reputation. They also need to stop being abused by people who get them for all the wrong reasons of threat and hard image. 'There are no such things as bad dogs, only bad owners' is a well-known phrase. It's not entirely true, of course, but it does apply to plenty of cases of Staffies. Dog shelters up and down the land contain more of them than any other breed, who just want to be loved and will pass on that love to anyone who does so.

So there was that thought again . . . we really should be doing the right thing and saving a beleaguered, ill-treated beast. It was settled and we agreed: 'This time we're definitely going to get a rescue dog.'

A few days later we noticed that our same Labrador breeder down in Devon had another litter on the way . . . Yes, we are empty, shallow people. All those good intentions and all just so much talk.

In fact, there was much about our second dog that was changed in the planning. Even when we had moved on from ideas of Staffordshire bull terriers or any variety of rescue dogs, we were then in line for another black Labrador. We had put our name down for a bitch again, and a yellow one if possible, but so had a few others and supply of yellows in this litter was limited. By the time we got onto it, still dithering over rescue dogs and our weak moral fibre, there was only one bitch remaining. She was black and that was fine – we knew that any dog from this litter would be great.

The single issue we had with another black one was that they do all rather look the same. Even though this seems on the surface the kind of statement that would only be heard in Labrador sitcoms of the 1970s, it does have more than a ring of truth. I had even had experience of grabbing Olive from a melee of dogs on a walk once and eased her out with a gentle boot to her backside while shouting 'Come ON – get MOVING' before realising that Olive was fifty yards away and it looked to all concerned that I was both abusing and stealing somebody else's dog. So the notion of getting an entirely different colour had been appealing.

Then, a call came in from Helen to say that another owner-in-waiting, a farmer in Devon, had generously offered to take the black one instead, leaving us free to have a yellow.

This is why I often sit Mabel down and tell her what her life might have been. If she is misbehaving or demanding then I take her to one side and let her know that somewhere her sister is working her little paws off at the crack of dawn going through her list of farmyard chores before breakfast and that it could have been her, so she should be grateful. I am sure that non-yellow Mabel is having a grand life as well, but it would have been very different with us.

Now, of course, we wonder how we could possibly have had any dog other than Mabel. But then, we would have been saying that about the second black one as well. Whichever dog you get, they very quickly become the only one you could ever have imagined owning.

As for the naming, this time 'Mabel' was chosen quite quickly. From the Latin meaning 'beloved', but more importantly two syllables and what we thought was an older lady's name. Although one of my friends now has a daughter called Mabel and with the young English singer of the same name, it's heading for a resurgence in popularity. How many newborn female human siblings will be named 'Olive' and 'Mabel', only time will tell.

Anyway, Mabel was from a huge litter – twelve puppies in total. The largest I can find on record in the UK was a litter of fifteen from a black Labrador called Annie in Campbeltown in the west of Scotland. I'm told that Annie subsequently became a nun and took herself away to a dog convent. Apparently the world record for the largest litter of any dog is a frankly absurd twenty-four – a record held by a mastiff, which, when you consider the size of mastiff puppies, makes the feat even more extraordinary. The mother could, at least, have used her pregnancy to steal vast quantities of food with the justification that she was eating for two dozen.

But twelve is still large. Very large. So when we travelled down to Devon again we were greeted by quite a sight. The mother, Izzy, appeared shocked by the entire experience and not a little drained. Olive's father Henry was also there – since we had last seen him he had fathered a few more litters and was ambling around looking reasonably pleased with himself and his life.

Helen looked a bit fatigued by the whole affair as well, but there was obviously some compensation. If you think about the price of a pedigree Lab at £750 per puppy[3] then a litter of twelve can ease the burden of caring and catering for something approaching a scene from *101 Dalmatians*.

I suddenly remembered Olive's litter with only four in total which can't have gone down too well. I also recalled a friend who had tried to breed from his dog with grand plans of helping to pay off his mortgage. The dog then managed to crack out one solitary puppy with an almost apologetic look as if to say, 'I'm really sorry, but that's all there is. Can we arrange some sort of bridging loan?'

Anyway, there they were, eight black and four yellow small, furry balls. It's one of the curious things about Labrador colours – two black parents can produce either black, yellow or chocolate puppies. It all depends on what the recessive genes are doing. Two yellow parents, by contrast, will produce only yellow puppies.

---

3. For a pedigree Labrador you would be more likely to pay around £1,000 now. £750 was the price of Mabel and Olive had cost £600. Mabel does occasionally like to remind Olive of this fact.

And you may think that since all three main colours can come from one litter that they would be pretty much the same under the fur, but not so – it's well recognised that the different colours have different characteristics and personalities. Perhaps not such a huge gap between black and yellow, but chocolate Labs (a very popular choice now) do represent a slightly more frenzied branch of the family tree. The common theme appears to be that whatever shade a Labrador might be, they are all remarkably cheery and optimistic dogs.

But with Olive and Mabel, the similarities end there.

19. Different Strokes

Nature or nurture? It is one of the eternal debates on the reason why people, or animals, have their own particular personalities. But I suspect that Mabel is the product of a conditioning process which has been going on from a very young age. Helen freely admitted that she had welcomed Mabel on to her lap quite often and, perhaps as a result, she is the most tactile canine in the history of human–dog relationships. It was very clear from the start, on the long drive back north, that whereas Olive had been happy enough in her box on the floor of the car, Mabel made constant applications to be a little bit more involved with whoever was in the passenger seat. Occasionally, as we hurtled along the motorway, she decided that she might like to try the lap of the driver as well.

Not that this was overly annoying and she was generally well-behaved. Although one other unfortunate, but quite noticeable difference to Olive was that, within just a few hundred yards of her new home, Mabel decided that she could keep it in no longer and let it all flow on my lap, for about thirty solid seconds, while staring at me in a deeply contented fashion.

Thus relieved, she was in great spirits to meet Olive properly for the first time in the back garden. This is a crucial moment when a younger dog meets the incumbent. You hope that there is just a bit of a nip from the older one to let junior know the pecking order, but Mabel, like most puppies, was not great at reading the signals.

'Hi. I see that you have growled at me and snapped once or twice. I take this to mean that you would like me to assault you constantly and try to chew your ears for the next two months. Correct?'

She just wouldn't leave Olive alone. And Olive, having enjoyed four years of peace and solitude, was clearly rather put out by the visitor, with those Labrador eyes that tell all and at that moment asked, 'Is this thing going to be staying for long?'

I'm pretty sure that from the start Mabel saw Olive as some sort of replacement mother. They are, in fact, related in that curious mixed-up dog dynamic, where romantic liaisons are free and easy and they don't feel tied down by human constraints or propriety. Olive's father Henry was also the father of another litter which contained Mabel's mother Izzy. Working it out, that makes Olive a half-aunt to Mabel, if there can be such a thing. One of these days we'll get everyone together on a Jerry Springer-style programme and Henry will be confronted by his numerous partners and offspring. Child support will finally catch up with him and it will all get messy.

One thing which was obvious was Mabel's love for Olive and within just a few weeks some, if not all, of that love was reciprocated. Neither would now want to be without the other, but again Olive could probably spend time without Mabel more than vice versa. And other differences became quite clear as the time passed.

For a start, Olive is a destroyer – always has been. There is just no point in giving her toys unless they are constructed from strange materials developed by the Soviet Union at the height of the Arms Race. Otherwise you may as well throw her a £20 note covered in gravy.

The names of expensive items such as 'Tough Toyz' or 'Indestructa-Chew' will prove themselves to be significant misnomers in the face of a determined Labrador. Anything remotely cloth-based will be slowly and methodically dismembered – the ears of the poor creature usually going first, followed by tails and feet until the fibrous entrails are pulled out in little clouds. In a box on top of our fridge there is a grotesque graveyard of ducks, snakes, pigs and foxes, all looking as if they have recently returned from the frontline of some futile stuffed-animal war. Appendages missing but still with their smiles fixed in place, despite the horrors they have seen.

Mabel is entirely different – she treasures her possessions. As a puppy she would bring things in from the garden – a twig, a leaf, a small flower and just keep them with her in her bed in a rather pathetic pile which, nevertheless, gave her great pride. Occasionally even now she will wander in from a walk, her cheeks just a fraction puffier than they should be and give the game away by looking ever so slightly pleased with herself. She also cracks immediately under the pressure of interrogation. Ask her, 'Do you have something?'

and her ears will slide back down to her shoulders while she shifts uncomfortably from paw to paw, making confessional noises before a piece of stick is extracted. In fact, Mabel will confess to anything – even if she hasn't done it. Many's the time I suspect Olive has been the culprit for misdeeds, but while she has kept her cool and looked slightly appalled that you have even suggested she might have done such a thing, Mabel crumbles and admits guilt just so that we can all start getting along again.

Her guilty face was perhaps best displayed on an occasion when she most certainly was the culprit during a short but dark period in her youth – the same one that Olive had gone through – when she decided that every night she would like to remove the stuffing from all beds and cushions.

I like to believe that she was initially uncertain but was encouraged during the small hours by Olive, who would tell her, 'It's fine. In fact, I remember from my own time that they really appreciate it.' Only when I came down in the morning did she realise that it wasn't in any way fine, as she sat amidst the debris, her low-wattage head trying to come up with an excuse but managing nothing more than, 'Look what happened . . .'

But now Mabel destroys nothing. In fact she has what they call in the gun-dog business a 'soft mouth' – ideal apparently for being a proper retriever, fetching birds after they have been shot from the sky. There is absolutely no chance of anything like that happening with us since I can't understand the desire to shoot anything, but Mabel clearly has greater retriever instincts. She will not only (with no real training) bring something back to drop at your feet, but she will also have tenderly cared for it en route, with just the gentlest hold for fear of damaging it, perhaps even trying to nurse it back to full health. Olive, by contrast, would be useless out in the field. She would take any wildfowl that had plummeted from the skies and wonder why she shouldn't just have it for herself. Then it would be carried off into the trees, where it would be steadily devoured before she rolled in the remains.

Indeed, after I posted a video which showed Mabel bounding into the long grass, so impressed was one country lady with her form that she asked me on Twitter, 'Do you work them?' and I wondered if she would accept as employment being a creator on YouTube. But I'm told that Mabel as top hunting dog goes against the grain. Among the shooting fraternity black Labs are considered the best, with yellow next and chocolate Labs borderline untrainable – the hyper and unteachable child. Ours are very willing to be educated – it's just that we haven't got round to it properly and, as a consequence, Mabel tends to take most of her guidance from Olive, her idol. Not initially in the least bit interested in eating grass, the student is now catching up with the master in the quantities she can devour, while proving equally inept at trying to pass it some twenty-four hours later.

What's more, I'm not entirely sure that Mabel is even aware of her own name. Quite often, when shouting it repeatedly, as I try and get her to stop whatever wrongdoing she might be up to on a walk, she will briefly raise her head and look around, as if searching for another dog, with an expression that says, 'Goodness . . . *somebody's* in trouble. I wouldn't want to be Mabel right now.'

Another key difference is that Mabel matured physically more quickly than Olive (mentally she is still playing catch-up after four years). Her first season actually took us by surprise as it came about a full year before Olive had got her womanly act together. Once again there were a couple of weeks of fending off the attentions of gentlemen callers and I became the protective father. So protective that I would always ask any other dog walkers if theirs were boys or girls. Although for some reason I felt I should use the proper terms of dogs or bitches when I was doing the enquiring.

This did lead to me shouting 'ARE THOSE DOGS?' at a man while pointing at creatures which were, to him, quite obviously dogs. He replied 'Ummm . . . yes, yes they are', before moving off, slightly quickening his pace.

Yet despite her physical advancement, Mabel is still, mentally, forever young and mildly idiotic. Often during the day she will decide that the task at the very top of her to-do list is to take one of those possessions which she so loves and start throwing it around, or rolling on her back, perhaps trying to hold it aloft and generally dancing to a tune that plays only in her head. This will go on for some time and usually finishes when she realises that everybody is watching. Throughout it all Olive carries a weary expression, as if witnessing Aunt Barbara on the dance floor at a wedding after a couple of glasses of Prosecco.

One other distinction between the two is the type of noises that they both issue as they try and make themselves understood. In fact I'm sure that the question which has been asked most often since the dawn of dog-human relationships is 'What do you WANT?'

And I imagine that we get it wrong quite a lot of the time. Even Lassie might have found herself deeply frustrated on occasion – galloping up to Timmy and barking her head off as the little chap asked 'What is it girl? The abandoned mine?' then led the towns-folk off on a rescue mission while a bewildered Lassie carried on barking 'Where are you all going? I just said that I'd been sick on the bedroom floor.'

Olive can be equally hard to read – giving vague whinnies that tell us she wants something. Quite what that something might be we can never work out and she perhaps doesn't even know herself.

She just wants stuff to be given to her and can't really understand why you aren't doing so. Mabel, though, is an open book. One with very large print and easy to follow diagrams.

She chats away in her near-constant demands for that contact and affection and you don't even have to touch her to start her off. The merest glance in her direction and her ears will go back, her whole body will start to wag and she will produce a series of squeaks and purrs at the prospect. Likewise, for the morning greeting she simply does not stop – padding around and singing one of her original compositions, specially written for the occasion. The lyrics expressing her worries that she thought she might never see you again, even though you went to bed only five hours ago.

Yet, despite all this chatter, our junior member of the household hardly ever barks. She saves that for very rare occasions on walks, when a male dog might try and get a bit handsy, or she sees a person with a hood up, which she doesn't fully understand. Otherwise she does all her speaking through an assortment of high-pitched utterances and some sort of interpretive dance based on her ears.

Olive, by contrast, does like to shout – and when she barks, at least, there is absolutely no room for misinterpretation, producing a very different sound for different events. There is that bark which she uses to summon us in the morning once her patience has run out – it has something of the mournful about it, as if expressing her sorrow that it should have come to this. Then there is the joyful throwing back of the head with her front paws up on the gate as I arrive back in the car, flapping her ears between happy cries, letting everybody know that life is good. Or there is the one produced at the same gate telling any passers-by who might be enjoying a pleasant stroll to fuck off and keep on fucking off, only letting up once they are out of sight. At which point she will trot back into the house in quite a perky fashion, satisfied with her work – leaving Mabel staring into space, looking a little bit shocked at the language.

But perhaps the most obvious difference between the two is that Mabel is obsessed with human contact. Let's not get Olive wrong – she's not cold-hearted in the slightest. If she is feeling particularly affectionate she will come and sit quietly beside you, perhaps the merest hint of a lean against your leg. She does have her weaknesses as well and is very partial indeed to a vigorous scratch around her tail-base, whereupon she loses a bit of her hard-earned dignity. But Mabel has never lost her dignity because she never had any to start with. She wants human hands upon her and what's more she wants to be upon you if at all possible, and she's not going to be ashamed of that.

In fact, once she has got those human hands in action she is very reluctant to give them up. If you are idly scratching an ear or stroking a chin beside you and stop, momentarily, you will swiftly feel the tap of a cold, wet nose or a full snout getting leverage under your arm with the message that, having given it some thought, she would very much rather that you continue.

So Mabel does on occasion stray into overly needy territory and yes, we have perhaps created this monster ourselves – or certainly nurtured it – but it is very hard to resist and if we both benefit from the deal then why change it?

And indeed there's nothing that we'd want to change. We realised, within a few months of getting Mabel, that we now had two dogs who looked and sounded very different, with very distinct personalities and character traits, but who complemented each other perfectly and who, after the initial misgivings from Olive, probably couldn't imagine being without their friend. We certainly couldn't imagine being without either of them – it seems so natural to have two.

But two is quite enough. For now.

20. Fishers, Farmers and Nobility (The Origins of Labradors)

If you were asked to draw a dog, the chances are that you would come up with something which looks a bit like a Labrador. So classically dog-like are they that you might imagine they have been around for thousands of years – sitting at the side of pharaohs, or perhaps being momentarily distracted as their Cro-Magnon owner was trampled by a mammoth.

But of course, like most breeds, Labrador Retrievers – to give them their full title – are actually a fairly modern incarnation of the dog genus, not officially recognised until the Kennel Club of the United Kingdom did so in 1903.

If you were paying attention in Geography, it should be fairly obvious that Labradors have their origins in the Canadian region of Labrador. While much of humankind was migrating in the other direction, the forebears of the Labradors made their way west to east across the Atlantic.

So I apologise for misleading you earlier with my suggestion that they were named after a Spanish nobleman. But interestingly there is a ring of Iberian truth to my nonsense, since Labrador itself is widely believed to have been named after the Portuguese explorer João Fernandes Lavrador (*lavrador*, incidentally, being Portuguese for farmer, while *labrador* is the Spanish equivalent).

The naming of places during the colonial land-grab is fascinating. The rules appeared to be:

1. If you were an expedition leader, you could let ego take over, turn a blind eye to the very obvious native people staring at you from the shore and name it after yourself.

2. You might decide to recall your own beloved country, perhaps using the prefix 'New' and imagining that you are enjoying the relative comforts of your homeland as you stave off dysentery or get mauled by a bear.

3. If you were a crawling networker with social aspirations, you named it after your patron, or the king or queen – often one and the same.

4. Then there were those who settled in a new found land and just couldn't be bothered. Hence Newfoundland. Perhaps they were tired after the long journey and it saved on the paperwork.

The various people who were already well aware of this terra nova might have questioned the name, but the reason I bring up Not-Really-Newfoundland is that the Labrador Retriever is more precisely from here than that adjoining part of the mainland called Labrador. It seems the history of this dog is littered with misnomers.

The one part of it which is certainly true is the retriever aspect. We think of them as being used out in the field to bring back pheasants, ducks or grouse or whatever might have been shot from the sky and that is certainly how they later developed in Britain, but back in their old country it was in fishing that they found gainful employment. These dogs would be flung into the freezing North Atlantic (remember those magical waterproof coats) to help pull in nets, or catch fish that had got away. Perhaps they would then exaggerate the size, telling tales with their paws a good three feet apart in the local tavern that night. Even though they do love to swim and were always keen to please, it must have been hard work – another thing I might tell Mabel when she's complaining that her breakfast is ninety seconds behind schedule.

One of the types of fisher-dog was the giant and distinctly furry Newfoundland breed, while the other was a slightly lighter breed known as either a St John's or a water dog and it is this smaller one that was eventually brought across the sea to start the lineage of the modern Labrador.

This ancestry is clearly why Olive and Mabel will rarely pass anything bigger than a puddle without wishing to dive in. Knowing their history, it makes perfect sense as I watch the two of them paddling furiously after a tennis ball in the sea or a river, something deep in the recesses of their brains telling them to chase down this errant sea-creature and bring it back to the boat.

And so it was the fishing trade which brought those Labrador prototypes to Britain with Poole, in Dorset, being a main point of entry. From here nobility stepped in and the rise of the Labradors really began.

The 2nd Earl of Malmesbury, who plied his lordly trade near Poole, realised that these immigrant dogs might be ideal for retrieving game while out shooting. Early in the nineteenth century he was doing just that and he actually called them Little Newfoundlanders, on account of the fact that they were smaller than the Newfoundland breed. His literal naming procedure would have been well received back over the water.

It was his son, the 3rd Earl of Malmesbury, who first decided to call them Labradors and they were clearly becoming quite desirable among the landed gentry, described by the Earl in a letter to the 6th Duke of Buccleuch as having 'a close coat which turns the water off like oil and, above all, a tail like an otter', and in the 1880s the Duke was given a couple of the pure-bred Malmesbury dogs to romp around the Scottish Borders.

Sadly, non-black Labradors were less desirable for work in the field in the early years. Therefore any yellow ones, or those which were classed as liver-coloured, which occasionally popped up in a litter, were likely to be quickly disposed of. It wasn't until the final year of the nineteenth century that the first yellow Labrador, 'Ben of Hyde', was registered. We even know that his parents were both black and were called Neptune and Duchess, and we have this detail because those responsible for creating and nurturing the breed really did like to take notes. Similarly to those involved in equine bloodstock, dog breeders don't seem to tolerate vagueness when it comes to who begat whom. And besides, since Labradors had become the favoured dogs of the nobility, their owners had the means as well as the desire to properly record them.

This aristocratic connection is also why we have photos of very early Labradors. There is a picture of Nell, owned by the Earl of Home, taken in 1867. Aged about eleven, she has a grey muzzle and paws but even in a grainy picture looks like any Lab you might see today.

Similarly a picture of Buccleuch Avon, owned by the 6th Duke of Buccleuch, shows him reclining in later years, having done the very important work of beginning the pure strain of Labradors that we know today. There is even a photo of the aforementioned Godfather of Yellows, Ben of Hyde, lying on the grass and looking hungry. If those nineteenth-century aristocrats had had access to a smartphone no doubt they would have had thousands of photos and videos clogging up the memory, just like mine. Those who love their Labradors seem to have been as devoted to them 150 years ago as we are today.

And over the intervening decades, the popularity of the Labrador only increased – the first dog to grace the cover of *Life* magazine was a Labrador called Blind of Arden in 1938. As far as I can make out he was being recognised for his triumphs in fetching and retrieving game – essentially granted the cover on the world's most famous magazine at the time for being a good dog. But, I suppose, for all dogs that is seen as the ultimate accolade and Labradors would surely collect the award more than any other breed.

They have proved themselves to be the best of companions to the human race and, of course, are still working today when required – invaluable as guide, therapy or assistance dogs. There are those who will perform tasks around the household for owners who might struggle: opening or closing doors, helping to dress or undress, raising the alarm, picking things up, even emptying a washing machine – although folding and ironing skills remain limited. There are Labradors who offer assistance to those with conditions such as autism, or can even, remarkably, alert owners with epilepsy that a seizure is imminent. Then there are those dogs whose job may be simply offering friendship as a member of the family, which, of course, is no less important. And where once only a select few knew of their credentials, now almost everybody is aware that with a Labrador you really can't go wrong.

They have been the dog of choice for so many notable people – far too numerous to list, but including Prince William and his hound Widgeon; Buddy, the sidekick of US President Bill Clinton during his time in the White House; and Konni, who often attended staff meetings and no doubt tried to offer some calming and sage advice to her boss, Russian President Vladimir Putin. We will draw a veil over the episode when she was used to try and intimidate the dog-phobic German Chancellor Angela Merkel.

How recent in the grand scheme of things the line of Labradors is, but already with such a long and rich history. It is fascinating to know how they came to be – how it started with those hardy dogs on the other side of the Atlantic Ocean, those fishing and fetching, always eager-to-please pioneers of the breed. How it led to adoption by the nobility and how they have sat at the right hand of dukes and duchesses, of royalty and world leaders.

And how it has all led to our own two beautiful dogs, both part of this great lineage. Beside me now one is lying on her back with her legs at assorted angles and jowls hanging down, the other snoring with the noise of a power drill.

I hope their ancestors would be proud.

21. Changed Times

Once upon a time, many years ago, we had nice things. Those halcyon days of clean furniture and smart clothing are now nothing but a distant memory. Please don't misunderstand me. In terms of companionship and all-round happiness, our lives have been transformed much for the better by Olive and Mabel – just for the state of our belongings a good deal worse. If you want to maintain a house to perfect, show-home standard, then Labradors are not a sensible option.

The vacuum cleaner runs permanently, but no sooner has it filled than the floor, sofas, dog beds and any exposed foodstuffs all seem to be covered in a veneer which is a blend of yellow and black. I can brush and brush the dogs with fur coming off in clouds and it makes no difference, except to our neighbours, as it drifts into their washing on the prevailing breeze. In particular with Mabel – save for a moult-free window of about four days in August – it just keeps coming, as if there is no solid dog beneath. I think if I were to persist in brushing for long enough, I could comb her away to just a nose, paws and blinking eyes.

We also now have no garments that are safe. In the days of only Olive, dark clothes were a good option as they didn't show up the fur which was inevitably plastered to them. Now they are claimed by thousands of little blond hairs and all items of clothing suffer.

Also, I'm not quite sure how it happened, but our house now seems to be constructed almost entirely out of dog-beds. You can barely move without tripping over one, as if they themselves are following my grandparents' dog-breeding programme. Olive and Mabel have their favourites, and use them on a rotating basis according to the time of day. Mornings in this one, then afternoon snooze here, evening on the bean bag. Overnight I fancy . . . yes, in THIS one. But then, quite often, all of them lie empty and unused as they stretch out on the sofas, occasionally kicking out with their legs as if trying to get rid of us.

The line is firmly drawn at our own bed, though. And by firmly, I mean really quite blurred. They might occasionally be invited up for a lie-in, but anywhere near the pillows is out of the question. I love these dogs dearly but have always been wary of those who would accept a lick in the face from one of their dogs while cooing 'Ooooo . . . Kisses for *Mommy*' when all parties involved know the awful truth of what that tongue has been doing just moments before.

And besides, when dogs are in the bedroom sleep is tricky. You might imagine that they slumber in a quiet and serene fashion when really Labradors – as we all do from time to time – offer an orchestra of noise throughout the night. Deciding that they aren't quite comfortable so turning around, then a flap of the ears, followed by the snoring at an international competition level.

And, in owning dogs, sleep is another thing I have come to miss. Again, this will be very familiar to those who have young children, but whereas children eventually reach the phase where it's impossible to get them up, with Olive and Mabel it's quite the opposite. Quite simply, our dogs are morning people.

Summers are the worst, when daylight creeps into the sitting room where they sleep, and at about 5.30 in the morning I can hear Olive going through her vocal warm-up routine – a series of low growls and very quiet yips that eventually lead to that full-on 'EVERYONE GET UP NOW BECAUSE THIS IS WHAT I WANT' bark.

The best thing to do is ignore her, but then I think of the neighbours and I stumble down the stairs in a wooden, middle-aged, what-in-God's-name-is-wrong-with-my-knees sort of way, to be met by the two bouncing happy souls, full of vim and vigour.

'*Great* to see you! What took you so long? I firmly believe that today is going to be AMAZING!'

The thing which irritates me most about it (and remember I am even more irritable through lack of sleep) is that after this early flourish our dogs – all dogs – then choose to sleep for much of the day. Olive will be immovable for most of the evening – 'Got to be ready to get you up at the crack of dawn!' Elsewhere in the dog world, I am told that greyhounds have a particular penchant for dozing, only being awake for something like four out of every twenty-four hours. Outstanding speed clearly comes at a price, but I envy their well-rested owners.

Yet whatever the breed of dog, they all have that very special gift of being able to switch from fully awake to comatose within seconds when it is what their minds desire. No brain whirring away, no worries about jobs or taxes or viruses or life in general – it's just a case of 'need to recharge now' and off go the lights. It does mean that we do get to see them asleep a lot, which provides its own entertainment as they enter their dreaming state. As I write this now Mabel is beside me on the sofa (uninvited) with her tongue poking out, eyes and nose twitching and her front paws starting to gallop. We obviously imagine that she is dreaming of all manner of great adventures, but she's probably dreaming of being asleep on the sofa.

I know that we should really dictate when our dogs do things, but if we're honest, quite often a day is entirely run by them. They are creatures of habit and they have come to expect and indeed demand certain things at specific points of the day.

When we first got Mabel we were firm about feeding time. Their evening meal was at 5.15 p.m., usually coinciding with the start of the quiz show *Pointless* on TV (there's a brief glimpse into the glamour of our lives). The regularity was such that, to this day, Mabel only has to hear the opening few bars of the theme tune for her ears to prick up, but really the enquiries begin long before that.

Despite the fact that she is generally greedier, Olive is much more relaxed about dining arrangements – she is a calmer dog in general and knows that it will happen, so why stress? Whereas for Mabel, stressing is a vital part of proceedings. She also believes that she can make most things happen with a firm enough stare – the impact of it is sometimes lost when she falls asleep in the process, eyes slowly closing, before jolting herself awake when her brain reminds her that she is on a very important mission. So she will fix us with a steely, occasionally dropping-off gaze for at least an hour beforehand – switching between whichever human she believes is more likely to provide and somehow fearful that if she doesn't do this, there will be no food and it will have been her own silly fault for not reminding us.

Then, of course, there are the requests/demands for walks. It used to be two walks a day until I made the mistake on one occasion of taking them out for a third, late at night. The next day around the same time they both sat, looking at me expectantly.

'Look, for as long as we can remember we have always had a third walk at quarter past ten. Now get your coat on.'

And it is on a walk that you realise how much your life really has changed as a dog owner. You see then that even if you thought you were in charge of them, it is quite the other way around and you dance to their tune now. Perhaps it strikes you most of all as they crouch with rounded back to unburden themselves of their very punctual breakfast or dinner and you wait to perform your menial but important task of keeping the countryside clean and tidy.

The greatest indignity is when you are stooping to pick it up, struggling to get it into the bag as one errant piece keeps escaping and meanwhile Olive (for it is always her) is covering you with leaves and bits of grass, doing that strange, post-defecatory celebration that dogs seem to enjoy, kicking it all up with her back legs. And I swear she's smiling as she does so.

'You enjoying picking that up, are you? Yeah . . . *pick that up*. Who's the master now?'

While I am talking about such indelicate matters, because of the enormous quantities of grass that Olive eats, sometimes she does not celebrate at all, because the whole process fails to run smoothly. Which only brings further indignity for us. You realise that something has gone wrong when she either fails to reappear from deep in the bushes, or you see her dragging her backside along the ground and waddling around looking at you with eyes that say, 'I'm not going to lie, this is not how I expected this to play out.'

So there you are, using a gossamer-thin bag as a makeshift glove, pulling away blades of grass which probably didn't envisage the last twenty-four hours playing out like this either. You pull and pull and this intricately-woven rope keeps on coming, like one of those never-ending handkerchiefs out of a magician's sleeve. Naturally, this is when a non-dog person walks round the corner and the sight that greets them is a sad Labrador in a crouching position and me bent over holding her tail aloft and rummaging around.

'Hi there! The JOYS of owning a dog!' I shout, in a manner that is supposed to be jovial but probably ends up suggesting genuine enthusiasm for the task and they shake their head in both pity and disgust before notifying the authorities.

If you are reading this as a dog owner I'm sure there are parts of it you recognise or understand. Or perhaps you are somebody who was thinking about getting a dog but is now reassessing your options and a cat is looking far more attractive.

All I would say is that, despite the fact that our house is not what it was and that the sofas are now a hue which Dulux might call 'Displeasingly Off-Beige' in their colour chart, despite the fact that all clothes are now made of a dog-hair blend and that getting more than six hours sleep is a thing of the past and the fact that their wants and needs can seem to rule our day, I couldn't imagine ever living that clean, tidy, sane dog-free life again.

22. Food, Glorious Food

Dogs have always pulled in big audiences on the internet.

A long time before Olive and Mabel did their thing I remember watching a series on YouTube which was mightily popular, where a Japanese owner set up an eating contest between her chocolate Labrador and two pugs. In each clip all three dogs are dressed up in costumes (I don't think it's mandatory in Japan but it certainly seems to be encouraged) and – spoiler alert if you haven't seen the videos yet – it doesn't end well for the pugs. At the start they sit in the wide-eyed way of their breed, looking appalled, as if having just been told a very inappropriate joke. Then the signal is given and the pugs are left still sitting, bewildered, as the Labrador destroys his own food, then theirs, then half a pug as well, such is the frenzy. All in all, it is an impressive display of greed.

To say that food is important to a Labrador is to rather understate things. Even if you weren't really aware of it you might have seen the evidence in the video which kicked all of this off, as Olive and Mabel inhaled their breakfast. As you may recall, taste was not of any importance – it was all about getting the food in before some forces unseen came and stole it from them.

In fact, Olive and Mabel would probably only be mid-table in the Labrador rankings for gluttony – which means they think about food for merely 98 per cent of their waking hours. Sadly for them (and very unjustly they would add), they only get two meals a day and I wouldn't say either of those is the most exciting culinary experience. We do, however, try and jazz it up by putting on a bit of a show. Every announcement of impending food is done by standing up and asking with a grand flourish 'Would you like . . .?' or 'Is it time . . .?'

I only include the start of these sentences here because that is all it takes. By now Mabel is throwing all the best moves in her dance of celebration with eyes that say, 'YES, I would like and of COURSE it is time.' But still you can see, as she scampers to her bowl licking her chops, that there is a hint of nervousness, fearing that I might change my mind at the last minute, wander off and never feed them again.

I'm told that dogs of a reasonable intelligence (and Olive and Mabel probably just scrape into this category, but would be holding the rest of the group back) can learn about two hundred words. They certainly recognise the words 'breakfast' and 'supper'. I tried to use the very Scottish 'tea' when talking about dinner, but it never really caught on. With their vocabulary only extending to about fourteen or fifteen words maximum I'm therefore not quite sure why I decide to chat away to them in the pre-amble to dinner, in much the same way that a maître d' would to a well-heeled party in a Michelin-starred restaurant.

'Have you selected from the menu, madam?' I begin, as I dig a sorry-looking plastic cup into a bin full of dry food.

'Perhaps a look at our specials? Today we have kibble and also a rather lovely kibble,' while I pick up their bowls, still greasy with licks from the breakfast service.

'I see . . . the kibble with a cold tap water jus . . . *excellent* choice,' as I try to get either madam to sit and wait, before all hell is let loose.

Every day it is the same offering, yet every day they enjoy it as if presented with the food of the gods. 'What's THIS? Kibble you say? Outstanding! You must give me the recipe . . .'

Of course, within twenty seconds it's gone and Mabel wanders happily around, thankful that her constant pestering and fretting paid off while Olive spends the next ten minutes attempting to lick through the bottom of the bowl and possibly the Earth's crust, grimly refusing to accept that it's all over. It's quite a performance for such a dull and repetitive meal.

That's not to say our dogs don't get a bit of variety. In the mountains, special treats of chicken or cheese may be administered and I changed Olive's life much for the better on another early climb by introducing her to a Marks & Spencer mini-sausage.

Very occasionally at home there might be something different as well – a carrot, or a bit of banana, or perhaps a segment each of satsuma, which Mabel will initially reject, letting it fall to the floor, but then perseveres for fear that news will get back to Labrador headquarters. We carefully investigate beforehand if dogs can even have certain foods as some that do us no harm are toxic to them. Onions and avocados are a no-go apparently and chocolate is ruled out for any number of reasons. One of the most notorious is grapes, but this is fine as we just leave them out of their Waldorf salads.

But what Olive and Mabel don't get is a constant supply of our own scraps – no leftovers find their way into their bowls. Sometimes I fear when visiting my mother that they might see how the other half lives, as she considers handing a plate to a dog merely a pre-rinse before it goes into the dishwasher. I close the kitchen door to spare our dogs the torment as giant Mungo and his sidekick Midge, a rescued Staffie, enjoy whatever is presented to them on the finest crockery. Olive stands, deeply suspicious that she is missing out, cocking her head at almost ninety degrees to try and better understand things, then whinnies her outrage and frustration.

When it comes to food, Olive is nothing if not a trier. She hangs around the bin, living by the Labrador edict that one should never give up hope and yes, occasionally a couple of peas have accidentally (entirely on purpose) made their way on to the floor. But really both of them have a certain element of discipline and self-control when it comes to our own food – they realise that there are boundaries which must not be crossed. We could leave the room with our dinner on a low-lying table and Olive, greatly tempted though she may be, will know that that way lies the telling off to end them all.

By contrast, up in Troon, Mungo would not even wait until you are out of the room and on several occasions he has seriously considered taking the food from a plate while you are still there eating it. Even in his limited mastiff cranium he is working things out: 'Get shouted at, but get pie. What is problem?' It is, rather fittingly for him, a no-brainer.

One of these days I suspect that Olive might also realise that the benefits will far outweigh any possible consequences. Not that she doesn't put the pressure on as we eat – Mabel will be fast asleep in her bed, her mind accepting that this is not their time, while Olive will stare, the tops of her ears and a black shiny dome just visible above the edge of the table. And eyes that fix upon you and say, 'Very slowly and calmly put the burger down on the floor and nobody need get hurt.'

But perhaps there is mitigation, as the constant quest for food might not be entirely their fault. Here's another science bit for you. In 2016, a study took place at the University of Cambridge, trying to get to the bottom of the seemingly bottomless Labradors. They examined a group of obese Labs and some more slender subjects and discovered that a genetic mutation in many of the chunkier ones meant that messages were not being passed to the brain to tell the dog that it was full. The study was then expanded to over three hundred Labradors from all walks of life and of all shapes and sizes and they found that 23 per cent of the dogs had this genetic flaw. And it seems to be that it exists only in Labradors and flat-coated retrievers. Of course, what this means is that 77 per cent have no excuse at all and are just greedy sods.

The serious point of all of this is that obesity in dogs is an issue in the same way that it is in humans. And just as it is with ourselves, we control what the dogs eat – give or take the odd bit of grass and whatever grimness they might find on a walk.

In the western world we love our dogs, but plenty of owners are in danger of loving them to death. Of course, it's hard to ignore their pleading eyes and think that 'he really wants this bit of steak/

bacon/Victoria sponge, so I'll just give it to him because it makes him happy'. The same dog will then end up waddling around, like a barrel with paws, out of breath and unable to enjoy so much of the fun stuff that dogs do, all because of the one activity that they seem to do better than any other.

But it's really not that difficult. Feed them less or exercise them more, because as much as they love their food, everybody knows – and we are about to discuss – that dogs are also more than partial to stretching their legs.

23. The Beach Girls

L et's get one thing straight. Dogs are happy with any walks. Through the lofty pine trees of Yosemite or down a filthy inner-city pavement – it's all good.

You will have seen examples of it many a time – a dog owner, cold and shivering, hood up in the pouring rain, misery personified. Beside them is their dog who bounces cheerily along, quite certain in its own mind that this is simply the *most* fun a dog could ever have had.

Olive and Mabel, though, really do have the greatest adventures.

Earlier in 2020, when all of us were restricted to more local areas, the walks did get slightly repetitive, but any boredom was more on our part than theirs. Blessed as they are with a combination of boundless optimism and sieve-like memories they would set off on every walk, every day up the same lane with, 'Hey . . . now *this* looks good!'

But in more normal times they have been utterly spoiled in the quality and variety of daily exercise which they receive. And it quite often involves a bit of sand beneath their paws, as beaches are the natural habitat of the dog. If your dog doesn't like the beach then I would suggest there is something wrong with it. It might not even be a dog.

Beach and dog – the two just go together. Even though we know they will appreciate any setting for a walk ('Lovely pavement – good to be alive, sir, don't you agree?!'), I think this is where most dogs are happiest and it's certainly where Olive and Mabel approach caffeine-fuelled cocker-spaniel levels of excitement.

Our go-to beach of choice is at Formby, just north of Liverpool – mountainous dunes and a vast expanse of firm sand, perfect for chasing balls. And the reason I know that the beach means more to Olive and Mabel than any other place is the difference we see, or rather hear, in them on the journey there. They are both, as a rule, very calm and totally silent in a car, but as we get nearer and they realise that the beach is going to be our destination for the day, little snippets of excited chatter start to emanate from the back of the car.

'Beach?' says one to the other.

'Yes, beach.'

'Thought so. We should let them know that we very much like the beach and are keen to get there.'

This begins when we are still a good ten minutes' drive away. How they recognise the intended destination, I don't know – perhaps familiar turns in the road, or more likely one particle in a thousand of sea air has come in through the air-vents, reaching their all-powerful noses, and so the conversation begins.

It means that by the time we drive into the car park they have reached excitement levels of approximately 13 out of 10 and when the tailgate opens no force on Earth can stop them. Mabel, in particular, will have attained a state of animation unknown to any creature other than a dog. I'm not sure there is any member of the animal kingdom which displays quite such a level of ecstasy over simply being outside.

Olive seems to care slightly more about holding on to her dignity, whereas Mabel has no such concerns. After exiting the car she starts the dance – a quite complex choreography where she rears up and spins round over and over again while at the same time managing to keep her eyes on the ball which, she hopes more than anything in the world, will soon be hers.

Because that is what our dogs do at Formby – from first moment to last all they care about are the balls, those things which will shortly try and escape along the sand and must, simply must, be caught. The humans have become mere blurry shapes and are relevant only as propellants of the balls. Still with eyes on the prize they skip backwards in a performance of dog dressage, bodies at a slight diagonal and perhaps losing marks for style by stumbling over rocks or piles of seaweed, such is the focus on the ball in the now blurry hands of the blurry shape.

Then away they go and the dogs are launched, always Olive first and then Mabel – two fur missiles bearing down on their targets.

It's here we discovered how fast they both are, because they are nothing if not committed – going flat out every single time a ball is unleashed. I once attached the GPS watch which I use for running to their collars and sent them each off on a pursuit of about 150 metres. Both reached top speeds of thirty miles per hour and I was the toast of Strava when I uploaded the results that night as one of my own sprint sessions.

You also realise that while they spend much of their time as cuddly, soft, doe-eyed and comical creatures, there is a wolf within – seeing the muscles straining, the manic stare and the bared teeth closing in on their quarry, you understand that our local squirrels should be grateful that they have never really got their act together.

Formby may be their regular beach, but they have not lacked for variety. Troon, as their home from home, and West Kirby on the Wirral peninsula also offer familiar scents. But they have gambolled, frolicked and swum on and around some of the finest beaches the UK has to offer. Claigan Coral Beach near Dunvegan on Skye or Sandwood Bay in Scotland's far north-west – both requiring a decent walk to get there but then rewarding you richly with the white sand and crystal-clear waters of that part of the world. Abersoch and Hell's Mouth in North Wales, Saunton Sands in Devon and Watergate Bay in Cornwall.

In pre-Mabel days Olive amused herself on the steep and pebbly beaches of Eastbourne when I was there covering tennis and on the same trip she looked down far too keenly at the shore from the top of the cliffs of Beachy Head. They have both bounced around in the Atlantic off Kintyre and the North Sea at Alnmouth and Bamburgh in Northumberland. They have recreated the opening titles to *Chariots of Fire* on the sands of St Andrews and have visited any number of beautiful coves and bays on island trips to Arran, Gigha, Raasay and Mull.

In fact, a small beach between Mull and the tidal island of Erraid, which appears only when the sea retreats, was one of the most memorable. The location features in Robert Louis Stevenson's *Kidnapped*, but more importantly for Olive it was where she first encountered seals. Four or five of them had come near to shore and with us the only other beings for miles around, the inquisitive creatures popped their heads up to see who the visitors were and what was going on. Olive, convinced that these were some dogs of the sea who were well worth investigating, and possibly had food to share, decided to bound into the surf and set off, swimming towards them. Perhaps, in her mind, she was back in the old country and was determined to land the catch of the day, hoping to be the talk of the Newfoundland inns that night.

Of course, she was misguided. She often is. Again, I would direct you to my Instagram account where you can see the video. It cuts off as I realise that this is unlikely to end well for her and that despite being a strong swimmer, she is, in so many ways, out of her depth. So I summoned her back to shore where she had a shake, quite happy in her own mind that she would absolutely have caught two or three of them if only we'd let her. Throughout the whole episode, and indeed the day, Mabel wasn't sure what was going on. I don't think she even saw a seal.

But beaches are most assuredly their favourite venue for a walk. It must be because of the sensory overload, the feel of the sand, the wind that whips up a thousand rich smells to assault their finely tuned noses. Because it offers sticks to chew and balls to chase or a flock of seagulls or waders to run towards, with the endless but hopeless thought that they might one day catch a couple who weren't paying attention.

And perhaps, most of all, because of that thing which laps at the edge of the sand and allows them to indulge in their all-time favourite leisure pursuit. Getting wet.

24. The Life Aquatic

Amphibious / am'fɪbɪəs / adjective
Relating to, living in, or suited for both land and water.
Examples: Common toad, Leaf green tree frog, Mexican
burrowing caecilian, Labrador retriever.

A s you might recall, if you have been paying attention,
Labradors are born to swim.

It usually doesn't take them long to discover water and furthermore to establish that they are very, very fond of it. Olive and Mabel
might have come to it by different routes, but the destination of
soaking wet happiness has been the same.

Olive, as mentioned, toppled into a canal as a puppy and we're still not sure if she meant it or not – but she certainly enjoyed the experience. Mabel, meanwhile, was in a country park, running in her crazed and less than coordinated fashion when suddenly we realised she was twenty yards out into a lake and she became aware that she was up to her nose in a thing which was cold and wet and different. And her world had changed forever.

But it was in Mabel actually learning to swim that the greatest joy came – both for her and for us. Although learning is not quite the right description since dogs just do it naturally. Or *fairly* naturally as the first attempts by Mabel were in obvious need of some refining. Again, the moment is on social media somewhere – Instagram, I think – as I stand in a river and she, desperate to get to me, sets off, thrashing her legs around, hammering at the surface of the water like an over-enthusiastic percussionist. It must have been galling for her that her very best efforts and slightly wide-eyed panic were met more with laughter than cheers. But I encouraged her all the way to reach me, whom she now viewed only as dry land and tried to scramble up my chest to safety. The livid claw marks were visible for a fortnight.

But how quickly she improved in technique and how much she loved it – even more so than Olive. And they had slightly different approaches to their water entry.

You may – or may not – have seen dog diving contests. If not, then it's worth an internet search and a subsequent hour or two watching hounds sprint down a runway before flinging themselves into the water in pursuit of a ball – marks awarded for distance and style. Once, we found ourselves at 'DogFest' – a giant dog festival, which is essentially just people with dogs, wandering round and observing other people with dogs, buying dog products and perhaps trying a dog-related activity or two. There, just such a competition was taking place, but there was no point in entering Olive as there was a sizeable crowd and it would only have meant humiliation for our whole family. While she does love to swim, she takes the slightly more cautious approach and doesn't do diving – she has to be able to feel the ground beneath her as she makes her way in. The sea, in her eyes, is perfect with a gradual and certain slope into the water.

Therefore, if forced into the diving competition, Olive would have reached the end of the runway and padded left to right, trying to shut out the cruel taunts of the crowd, staring at the ball and wanting it very, very much indeed but hoping that somebody else might be able to get it for her.

Often now that somebody is Mabel – in fact, only a day after her initial swimming efforts our junior dog showed she was made of sterner, or slightly more foolish, stuff. With a ball thrown into a pool, Olive was skipping nervously around on the edge, whining and half-pawing at the water in a futile attempt to drag both water and ball back to her when Mabel came flying past, running into mid-air above the water like Forrest Gump off the shrimping boat after he spotted Lieutenant Dan. And now she will jump in anywhere as Olive looks on, pretending that she doesn't care but secretly, I suspect, envying Mabel's have-a-go attitude.

Of course, it doesn't have to be swimming and it doesn't have to be in the sparkling sea or a beautiful mountain stream. Mabel, in particular, is a water-seeking missile wherever we might be. If the famous pond video hadn't worked first time, she would have needed little encouragement to go for another take. And it could have been filmed on any one of our walks. If there is water, Mabel will find it and either swim, paddle or stand in it – but usually a combination of all three.

Yet the curious thing to note is that despite Olive and Mabel's overwhelming love for water and the fact that on every walk they will try and engineer a situation where they are in it, when they get home and might need to be washed, there is no substance which they hate more.

If they have taken it upon themselves to spice up a walk by rolling in a pile of unmitigated awfulness, they quickly realise that something is afoot when we get back. Whichever dog is guilty might have thought it was going to be a triumphant return, where they are met with a guard of honour and applauded back into the house and widely lauded for their efforts, but when I don't immediately open the door for them and instead head round to where the garden hose is kept, they know that things are about to take a more sinister turn.

Now the criminal falls upon my mercy and engages full-on pathetic mode – ears down, tail curled firmly between legs – pleading that if I spare them this time, it certainly won't happen again, sir. And also, it wasn't really my fault because a bigger dog made me do it.

But it's too late and the sentence is carried out, as I first gently scrub the detritus of fox or bits of dead bird out of their strangely brown and matted fur, while offering soothing chat, 'Was this really worth it? Hmm?' Then, if the hose is simply too much to bear, I'll have to get a basin of water, tested for temperature, much as you might dip an elbow in before bathing a newborn baby. I remind myself throughout this process that I couldn't get these dogs out of a freezing pond five minutes ago.

We did even investigate getting a hot water tap installed outside. We heard from a friend that his spaniels were such supporters of the whole washing experience that, at the end of a walk, they formed an orderly queue by the tap, holding their towels and wearing shower caps.

But with Olive and Mabel it wouldn't have made a difference. You see, it's nothing to do with temperature or water pressure. In fact, it took me a while to work out why, but I did finally come to understand the reason behind them intensely disliking a bath, or being covered in water out of a hose when they love it anywhere else.

And the reason is? Well, it's quite simple. It's because our dogs are idiots.

25. Irrational Beasts
(And Where to Find Them)

If you're still reading, rather than having thrown the book aside in disgust at my insulting manner, I know that Olive and Mabel aren't idiots. Well, they sort of are, but I accept that, to them, their concerns are very real and must have come from somewhere. Even though we become frustrated at what seem to be irrational fears or worries, there will be some reason they feel that way.

To get briefly technical it comes down to the fear imprint stages of dogs. As they begin to grow more independent from their mothers and discover the world, anything which upsets them can be seared on their memory and forever cause them to reach for a steadying bottle of brandy.

The first stage comes around eight to twelve weeks, but then there is a second phase which arrives at about six months and can last up to a year or so beyond that. There might be the slightest incident which occurs during that time, and it may not even appear large enough to warrant the description of 'incident', but it can do something to some part of their furry little brains which has a permanent effect.

For what it's worth, I don't think the bathing thing is anything do with any occurrence during the fear imprint stage. That just comes down to the fact that they don't like bathing. Some dogs will happily climb into a bath, others will cling to the sides for dear life or merely stand, in their misery and suffering, the most sad and bedraggled creatures on earth.

But there are other fears, concerns and dislikes for Olive and Mabel which are so irrational and make *so* little sense that they can only come down to some traumatic, triggering moment in the dim (oh so dim) and distant past.

Let's run through a few of the things we might find in Olive and Mabel's Room 101.

OLIVE
1. The vets
2. Certain floors
3. The floor in the vets
4. Oscar, the cat next door
5. Mechanical objects in the sky
6. Ferries
7. Other people on a mountain

8. Baths and/or showers
9. Worm medicine

MABEL
1. The vets
2. Not being touched enough
3. People who are doing nothing
4. Selected other dogs
5. The beeps of a GoPro camera

So, where to start? Number 1 is fairly obvious and so familiar to all dog owners that we will deal with it shortly in a separate chapter. But let's examine the rest of the lists for each of our dogs:

OLIVE

2. *Certain floors*

This dislike is one of the most curious. Some fears I can understand – once, for example, while she was in the back of the car we were hit from behind by another driver. Not too serious an accident, but it did lead to her refusing to get into the car for three or four months afterwards. Fine – that makes sense. Yet where Olive's deep misgivings about specific surfaces come from I don't know. Perhaps once she was given really disappointing news while standing on some parquet flooring.

But it does lead to some awkward situations. Very few wooden floors in new venues meet with her approval, despite the fact that this kind of thing covers much of her own home. And it will take her two or three paw steps in through the door of a café before she decides that this is just not going to work for her. In entering one hotel, her angst and our desperation reached the point where I was moving rugs to make an acceptable surface, as if scattering rose petals in the path of royalty.

Linoleum is also often a no-go, but it has to be a very specific type. In one of my favourite outdoor stores, the floor changes in texture by just a fraction at some point and Olive refuses to go any further. Conveniently, it seems to leave her stuck in the section where the dog equipment display resides and she gets to do a bit of browsing.

Incidentally, bridges can have a similar effect, but that seems to be more when she can see through the gaps to the river or whatever it is below. Mabel will be trotting across quite happily while Olive goes low as if spreading her weight and inches her way to the other side, concerned that she will tumble through and be eaten by a troll.

3. The floor in the vets

It's just a double-whammy of awfulness. And no more needs to be said here. Moving on . . .

4. Oscar, the cat next door

This is not a fear, but rather a very strong dislike and I would say the feeling is mutual. Oscar is – and I say this with all due respect to our wonderful neighbours – a bit of a dick. Poppy, their other, more senior cat is lovely – genuine and straightforward, and when she says she wants affection she means it. Oscar lies to you. He is one of those aforementioned felines who calls you in like a siren, purring away, before attacking with a vicious left–right combination. He also clearly sees himself as massively superior to our two dogs, viewing them as slightly gormless. And yes, he may have a point. He therefore likes to sit on the roof of our shed and invite them to come and have a go. Olive does exactly this after she has either spotted him from inside the house, in which case she will launch herself at the window, steaming it up with a series of snorts and quite explicit language. Or I decide to tell her quietly that, 'Oscar is outside and are you going to stand for that?'

'Oscar', you see, is one of the fifteen or so words in the Olive lexicon and you only have to whisper it for the ears to elevate, the tail to shoot straight out and for the big talk to begin. And it is all talk, of course. If Olive ever got out there and Oscar were not on the shed but on the grass, having decided to stand his ground, then she wouldn't know quite what to do.

As it is, I suspect that both are quite happy with their role in this bit of garden theatre. Olive can do a bit of shouting and swagger around: 'You are very lucky to be out of reach, my friend, or you would be in a world of pain right now.' Oscar can flick his tail and look down on his nemesis both physically and metaphorically and both can then be happy that dog and cat honour has been satisfied.

Throughout it all, Mabel doesn't quite get it and skips out behind Olive, carrying a favourite toy, suspecting that she's supposed to be cross but happy just to be taking part.

5. Mechanical objects in the sky
Olive simply doesn't understand them. No more needs to be said than it makes no sense at all that they are up there and they should consequently be feared. She has a point.

6. Ferries
This one pains me because I *love* ferries and I wish she did as well. There was a time when Olive was quite happy on them – when she

was still quite young we went over to Arran in the Firth of Clyde and there was not a single issue. So something must have happened in the fear imprint stage. Perhaps on that trip she lost a significant amount of money on the fruit machines in the passenger Fun Zone. Or maybe it comes down to floors again, because she has clearly decided that the metal surface beneath her paws is not for her. As we leave the car deck and head up the stairs you can see her rising panic. Then, we get outside to where ferries are most enjoyable and she puts the brakes on to such effect that the collar pops up off her head. If a helicopter were then to come into view at the same time it would all get too much and she might fling herself overboard into the sea. And Mabel would applaud her technique.

7. *Other people on a mountain*

Again, I have some sympathy with her position as I do like to see nary another soul when we are out in the hills. Fortunately we do get to climb when few people are about, but it's still very rare that we don't see anybody. I think this might add to the impact for Olive as we will have been wandering around in our own company for hours and then there appears a distant speck or two, getting closer. Usually, since we start so early, they are coming up as we are heading back down and so they are struggling through the climb when the guardian of the mountain flies at them from about two hundred yards away.

'She's VERY FRIENDLY,' I shout, while trying to maintain an insouciant air, but my cries are often lost to the wind. Thankfully Olive backs up my words by dissolving into a wagging, licking mess when she reaches the people, if they haven't turned and fled. But in my experience people of the outdoors tend to be people of dogs as well.

Unfortunately, Mabel ruins the amicable vibe by remaining deeply suspicious, keeping her distance, letting out a very rare woof which seems to scare her as much as anyone (we'll deal with this shortly). Eventually I buy her silence with a sausage or bit of cheese. Which probably lets her know she's done the right thing and she'll be just as offensive next time.

8. Baths and/or showers
Misery for Olive. See previous chapter.

9. Worm medicine
This treatment is very necessary because of all the hideous things our dogs believe are well worth sticking their noses into and/or subsequently eating. And it's nothing really – just a little tube of liquid which is meant to be squirted on to their skin around the shoulders and neck. More often with Olive it just ends up in her fur because (a) you have to dig through about a foot and a half to even reach the skin and (b) she is very keen to free herself from this godawful situation and escapes just as you are squeezing the tube. As a result a great deal of the medicine ends up on my hands, but at least my fingers remain worm-free.

Such is her concern that she only has to hear the sound of a metallic blister pack being cracked open and it sends her scurrying to the corner. Therefore, if we ever need throat lozenges, ibuprofen etc, which are also contained within such packaging, they have to be opened out of her earshot.

Again, we have no idea why she dislikes it so much. We did wonder if it might burn the skin slightly, but then realised that no, it was just because her brain had taken against it for reasons unfathomable to us, but very important to her.

And besides, Mabel is fine with receiving her dose. Or at least she would be, but then she sees her friend and idol in distress and starts to worry that if Olive is upset then there must be something serious going down. But Mabel will quickly move on and forget this disturbing thought, as she has plenty of her own discomfiting issues to occupy her brain.

MABEL

2. *Not being touched enough*

It seems a trifling matter to open with, but it really does concern Mabel. As we have discussed, she is never happier than when she is being given human affection. The reverse of this is when she feels that she might be missing out. Any number of applications are then made to remedy the situation, involving a growl-purr-whine which makes her sound like Marge Simpson, or by presenting a selection of manky toys as part-payment for a stroke or a scratch. Eventually we give in and she lets out a contented sigh – all is right with the world, but it was a close-run thing.

3. *People who are doing nothing*

This is an odd one. Like all Labradors, Mabel is a people-person, but if those people are not acting in what she believes to be a conventional manner then she can't work it out. And let's be clear that 'unconventional' in her eyes might be somebody merely standing still. For her, when the line between human and inanimate object becomes blurred it is a distinctly unsettling experience.

The most striking example of this was when we took both dogs for a walk at Crosby Beach. It's now famous for the work by sculptor Antony Gormley called 'Another Place' – one hundred cast-iron figures spread out across the vast expanse of sand, staring out to sea and being alternately covered or revealed as the tide ebbs and flows. It is a beautiful and haunting work – needless to say Mabel was quite the critic, not questioning the finer points or deeper meaning, but simply wondering who all these people were and why they weren't moving. At the same time, Olive was asking them for biscuits.

4. Selected other dogs

Mabel is very sociable with other dogs, but only after they have been accepted into her close inner-circle of friends. More often, on meeting another canine, we see one of nature's great displays in her incredible rising fur. I obviously knew of hackles before we got Mabel, but she is a remarkably gifted exponent of the art of hackling and if there is any other dog who can hackle as well as she does, I'd be surprised. Perhaps they do occur on Olive as well, in particular in Oscar-based situations, but I've never seen them. Of course, with Mabel's colouring, they would be more visible. They are, as I believe I mentioned, quite the hackles.

Even in play-fighting with Olive as a puppy you can see that Mabel has her dark ridge of ferociousness. Have a look at that 'archive sports commentary' video of the two of them and it is there, if somewhat junior and pathetic. Now, as an adult, she wanders round like a stegosaurus when she believes the situation warrants it – which in her head is often.

This may sound like our junior dog is somewhat unhinged, or at least very nervous and troubled. Not so, but she does approach most new dogs with a wariness. It doesn't matter the size of the dog either – the rules of the game are unclear. It could be an inoffensive and cheery Bichon Frise and Mabel's thought process becomes vividly illustrated: 'Hmmm . . . not sure about this guy. I'd better make myself look enormous. There . . . everyone now shall bow down before me.' And then she's fine, until she sees a person who she thinks might be a tree and it all starts again.

One thing of which she is absolutely certain – she really does not care for the dog which has the absolute cheek to visit our garden, every night, just after dark. Most galling of all is that it comes right up to the window and is carrying her favourite toy. They stare at each other, evenly matched, neither giving an inch, until we close the curtain and Mabel retires warily to her bed, all of us fairly sure that it will return the following evening.

5. The beeps of a GoPro camera

Across the whole range of concerns for both of our dogs, Mabel's fear of the seemingly inoffensive beeps made by a GoPro Camera is the most dramatic. You may be wondering why I am being so specific about the make of camera and the reason is that Mabel is just as precise in what upsets her.

There are plenty of beeps in her daily life – every single electronic gadget in the house seems to be chirping away at some point and none of them makes the slightest impression. But a single sound from Satan's own filming device and she is in pieces. The way this was all discovered was that one evening I had been working on the camera, fiddling at its beepy controls, when we noticed that Mabel had disappeared. She was eventually tracked down hiding in an upstairs bedroom, possibly with her hackles raised but difficult to tell in the dark.

But again, this makes little sense because it is just that sound and only that frequency which terrifies her. One microhertz higher or lower and she's fine. Of course, dog hearing is a very finely tuned machine – they can hear sounds that we can't (like a dog whistle operating beyond the twenty kilohertz upper range of a human ear) and they hear things differently. Who knows, perhaps to Mabel the exact frequency of a GoPro contains a hidden message, like a 1970s prog rock album played backwards, telling her she's going to be taken to a dog pound, run by cats. If she only knew that the machine which makes her noise from hell is often strapped to her back, just with the beeps now disabled, she might think twice about being the camera dog in our latest filming projects.

But I hope you will have seen here how strange and unfathomable is the mind of a dog – even two as happy and cared for as Olive and Mabel. It should also be quite clear how their sources of angst vary – what terrifies one doesn't seem to bother the other in the slightest. But there is a matter upon which they agree: there is one thing, one location which bothers them – and almost all dogs – very much. Very much indeed.

26. The Place That Shall Not Be Named

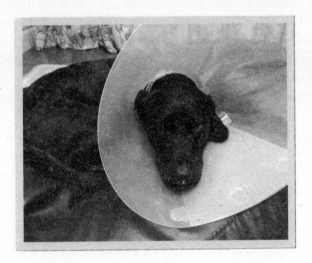

I can say the word to you, because you, dear reader, are not a dog. At least I presume not – surely even an incredibly gifted Border collie won't have got this far in the book. Or perhaps they would have, but were so disappointed in the laboured prose that they went off to round up a few sheep, while doing algebra.

But to all dogs, the word 'vet' is entirely unacceptable. Instead, every time we need to discuss the place, we rely on our dogs' inability to spell and perhaps even whisper it as an added precaution, just in case they now recognise the word vee-ee-tee.

Olive and Mabel are no different to the general dog population in this regard, although it wasn't always the case. Very early in their lives the vet was not scary at all – just another place to meet and mingle, with dogs to sniff, humans to say hello to. Labradors are, after all, the great networkers. As well as that, there might even be a cat, peering through the bars of a small carry-box and looking royally pissed off with the situation, which always seemed to amuse Olive.

But for both our dogs things changed after the operation to have them spayed. From the moment they staggered or were carried out, still groggy and feeling decidedly sorry for themselves, all matters vet-related were different. I do remember holding Olive's paw most of the way home in the car and apologising to her and there was similar guilt with Mabel. But from that point onwards in their lives, they recognised the vet as an abode of the damned for dogs, cats or whatever other poor creatures may have been dragged in there.

That's not to say that our two have to be dragged into the vets at all. In fact, they bounce in quite happily, glad to see one and all again. It's only when you take your seat in the waiting room that there is a slow awakening of memory – a gradual realisation that we are here for more than a few cheery hellos.

Olive does tend to handle it rather worse than Mabel. 'Oh bollocks . . .' you can see her thinking, as it dawns on her: 'I remember this place.' So you offer her a small consolation biscuit. Then somebody else does as well. And she is shivering and shaking so much, with her eyes turned up to full pleading mode, that she gets given snack after snack until you wonder if the vet is going to draw your attention to a chronic weight problem which she didn't have when she came in.

In her mind her tactic is clear. Every time the inner doors open to the actual consulting rooms, she reverses further and further under the chair – only a mouth occasionally appearing to gently take another biscuit and then retreat once more into the shadows.

Then comes the moment of reckoning – the vet appears and calls out 'Olive?' so beginning the hugely entertaining show for all other pet owners in the clinic. I will at least TRY and walk her in on her lead but know that we can probably just skip straight past this to stage two: me having to remove her sheltering chair-fortress and give her some soothing chat while asking her to please be reasonable.

'Come on, don't be so silly now. It's the briefest of check-ups and *look* . . . it's Susan, that vet you like.'

But really stage two is also a pointless charade and we are merely going through the formalities before stage three – lifting and transporting. She looks up at me with her ears disappearing and eyes that could melt the coldest of hearts, gently batting me away. By this point she has the watching room firmly on her side, oohing and ahhing and twisted round her little paw. So I try to cut through it all with a poor attempt at humour.

'God . . . it's as if she doesn't even *want* this nose-job.'

Now I'm starting to worry that everyone might think this poor dog is ill-treated at home and I'm also really trying to do a proper farmyard animal carry for fear that my lifting technique will be critiqued by the onlookers.

'Look at that, he's hardly supporting her back at all. Some people shouldn't be allowed to have dogs . . .'

By this stage, though, I've lost a bit of patience with her eyes-drawn-by-Disney and I'm more concerned about my own back giving way. Olive is not a huge Labrador, but still, twenty-six kilos of wriggling dog in a defensive formation will test your core strength. So we rather wrestle with each other and eventually

I get her up and into a position where she is clinging to my shoulder and shivering her way to the gallows. Mabel at least has the decency to be quite simply dragged in on the lead, head bowed in resignation and sliding across the polished floor.

It all continues within the consulting room and, indeed, once there, both our dogs are capable of escalating the situation. I almost have to admire their ability to find an extra gear of misery when I thought they were already operating at peak capacity. Again, Olive is prepared to put up more of a fight and with a lack of chairs to hide under she realises that her greatest ally is now the corner. And she has a point as I can't then get any arms around her to lift her onto the table. I try and explain to her that if she really wants the vet to give her the all-clear then shivering and panting as if in her death throes is probably not the way to go about it.

So eventually the vet comes to her and we can get on with things – Olive letting us know at all times how much she is suffering through this torture of being lightly touched and given biscuits.

But I do console them because despite the fact that they are being ridiculous, I know that the concern and upset is, in their heads, very real indeed. One thing it confirms for me is that when the final day comes, however nice everybody is who works here, I will not be bringing a dog in for their last moments. It will happen on a favourite bed in a familiar, happy and comfortable place and I will sell my own limbs if necessary to make it so.

Five minutes later we exit the abode of the dog-damned and all is well. Olive and/or Mabel desperately scrabbling towards the door of freedom, letting me pause only briefly to give the receptionist a sizeable sum of money and then they skip happily out into the world, to entirely forget once again about the sheer awfulness of this place – chuckling at an imprisoned cat as they go.

So let us take them, and you, away to a happier environment – far from the antiseptic and the deeply probing thermometers and the walls which close in and return instead to the wide open spaces of the mountains, which are airy and free and where it feels as if we could walk forever. But, of course, first you have to get there.

27. The Trip

It's very fortunate that the mountains are only five or six minutes away by car from where we live. Unfortunately this is only fact according to Olive and Mabel, since on the actual journey of perhaps two or three hundred miles, they will spend 99.5 per cent of it asleep.

As I grapple for hours with a sore back and fighting the demons of roadworks and middle-lane drivers on the motorway, they remain unconscious and consequently believe that everywhere we go is just around the bend at the top of our road.

As we have mentioned before, falling asleep is not a task which they find particularly demanding and they are assisted in their efforts by the fact that they travel in the grandest of luxury, with the whole boot kindly donated. Olive might grumble that things were better in the old days when she had the place to herself, but even with two beds in there, there is room to sprawl.

I'm glad they're not the constantly yapping or whining dogs that some owners will have to endure on car journeys and I do like the idea of them being comfortable, but it does mean that we perform the neat trick of taking a big car and making it incredibly small for our own needs.

When we are going away for a couple of days or longer, our luggage and everything else we need is piled high on the back seat, squashed in behind us or poking through over the arm-rests, all so that Olive and Mabel can enjoy their fully extendable, first-class flat-beds.

Once, in pre-Mabel days, I did give half of the boot over to a giant equipment bag, but still with more than enough space for Olive to travel in great comfort. On arrival, though, I found that she had sacrificed some of her sleeping time on this journey to chew through one of the straps, rendering it impossible to carry forever more, and she met my outrage with a face that said, 'I'm not even sorry – don't let this happen again.'

I did mention that the dogs are usually comatose for the vast majority of any long journey and the fraction that is otherwise comes when I force them awake at a service station. I open the tailgate to be greeted by their slightly rumpled faces – Mabel often with a confused look and a small bead or two of drool on her muzzle – and insist that they get out.

They are almost as familiar with the dog-walking area round

the back of Tebay services (about ninety dog-seconds or so from where we live) as they are with the lane outside our own house. Generally, dedicated dog-walk areas are to be avoided, but at motorway services you have little choice – usually it's just a tiny patch of grass available on the fringes of the car park. Because every other dog owner has also had little choice, you tiptoe around in this minefield, all the while making cajoling and encouraging noises in the desperate hope that your dogs will do something and you can finally go and get an average cup of coffee.

'Good GIRRRRRRLLLLL!!!!!' you say, in a voice which is a mixture of gratitude and wonder, as if she has just solved Fermat's Last Theorem rather than crack one out behind somebody's camp-ervan. And she looks at you as you cheer her on, slightly embar-rassed for both of us. But after doing what they have to do they then hop back in, I offer each of them a small biscuit like an air steward bringing round the snack trolley and they settle down once more. It can only be a matter of time before they insist on screens to entertain them during the journey.

One thing they have never tried while travelling by car – possibly because the opportunity has never presented itself – is the classic dog-head-out-of-the-window thing. I suspect they would like to and I'm sure they have heard tell from other dogs about the joy of it – ears flapping and tongue hanging out with eyes closed and feeling the breeze in their fur – but they just never get the chance.

Some of that is due to over-caution on our part, a fear that a head out of the window would somehow meet a tree branch, or a cyclist, or a lorry or perhaps even a dog doing exactly the same thing coming the other way and – remarkably solid though Labrador heads are – it might not be great for them. But it's also because Olive and Mabel simply can't get near the back windows with luggage enough on the back seat to suggest we are not so much going on a climbing trip as moving house.

And I should say here that a lot of that is their fault as well – because of everything they need in the hills, straining the equipment bag with the chewed-through strap. So when we arrive at our climb, it is always a cause of some resentment as they hop out, refreshed and raring to go and now whining that I am taking too long and depriving them of this walk and also why don't we come here more often since it is so *close* to our house. I stretch and then stretch again, then realise that this is probably as good as it is going to get and start to load my rucksack with all of the things which they need. So before I tell you about Mabel's first proper day in the mountains let me go through the list of items – essential and otherwise – that will weigh me down over the next few hours.

28. The Pack and the Pack Horse

First of all I should say that I perform my load-bearing duties willingly. Even if it's clear that Olive and Mabel enjoy a day in the hills, they haven't specifically requested it and, what's more, with their imbecilic running, both hither and thither (mostly Mabel's role) they are going to be climbing a far greater height than me. Yes, it's possible to buy dog jackets that drape over their backs with pockets attached so that they can carry some of their own things like a mule, but I want to make life as easy as I can for them.

So on goes the rucksack – and I instantly find myself bending forward, like a Himalayan porter. And I question my manhood as I do, straining under fifteen kilos as they might do beneath sixty.

Let's start with the rucksack itself. Not a huge one, usually forty litres – or seventy if I have ambitious and foolish plans of camping in the hills. Contained within, as well as normal human accoutrements such as crampons, poles, ice axes, camera, gloves, hat and extra layers, come the following canine items:

1. *Water bottles and drinking bowl*
Olive will drink from mountain streams, but only if it is her idea. She cannot be persuaded. Fortunately Mabel is entirely suggestible in all aspects of life and you can quite easily lead her to water AND make her drink. However, in winter any water source may well be frozen or covered by snow. Both Olive and Mabel are deeply fond of eating snowballs, but as any winter survivalist should know, they offer nothing in the way of hydration.

2. *Dog coats*
As previously discussed, if the temperature with windchill is going to get somewhere below minus ten or so, then I would put them in a coat. They are not garments worn with any great pride and do increase the shakes and scratches of irritation, but it eases my mind knowing that they can't possibly be freezing and so are well worth the cripplingly large amount of money spent on them.

3. *Lead*
One of the most important items. Ideally one with a bit of stretch in it, so that when your dog does get the scent of something very special which requires immediate investigation, then you're not pulled off your feet. More seriously, on the lower slopes of most

mountains sheep are often to be found and farmers are well within their rights to shoot a dog it if is worrying a flock, especially if they are pregnant ewes.

I am usually very diligent and responsible in such matters. But I do regret that on one occasion when I thought the coast was clear, Olive detected that a white rock up ahead was moving and the chase was on. Already coming off second-best in the race, the sheep lost its footing and Olive was quickly upon it. Yet, being rather useless and far from a killer, she didn't know what to do next, so just stood by her quarry until the sheep was able to get back on its feet. They then stared at each other for a moment – neither really sure as to how they should take it from here and eventually the sheep continued on its way.

A lead is also vital for the more extreme parts of a mountain in snow, where a dog, oblivious to how things like cornices work, could easily fall through and still be scratching their heads, trying to puzzle it all out as they tumble into the abyss (see chapter 29).

4. Tick comb

Obviously not enormous in weight and not relevant on a frozen winter climb, but worth mentioning as a vital piece of equipment. Ticks are deeply unpleasant and dangerous to both dogs and humans, leaping on to any unsuspecting host and digging in for their parasitic fun – possibly passing on Lyme disease in the process. A tick comb is therefore very necessary, not to give the unwanted visitor a natty side-parting, but to twist and remove the creature without leaving the head still latched on. It is a curiously satisfying procedure to perform, yet despite the fact that both Olive and Mabel are frequent visitors to undergrowth which would be a tick-hotbed, we have only rarely encountered them. I'm led to believe that they are often unsuccessful with Labradors, so luxuriant is their fur. Perhaps they hop on, dig away for half an hour before giving it up as a lost cause. Or possibly they tried it with Mabel's head and kept on digging until they found themselves coming out the other side having never encountered anything more substantial.

But, of course, there are plenty of less furry areas to attack, which leads to the very important 'tick-check' of an evening which both dogs seem to rather enjoy. In fact, you can thoroughly inspect Mabel top to toe and when you're finished she will demand further examination, acting out the symptoms of Lyme disease for effect, suggesting that you may have missed a spot and would quite like to be touched again.

Last, but probably most importantly on a climb, we find a whole lot of . . .

5. Food

About a third of the weight in my rucksack usually comes from provisions for the day. Add in dog sustenance and it increases to a half. I know how much I have to eat to fuel the effort in the mountains, so the dogs will be the same. And as well as the usual dog biscuits, a mountain is a place to have food not otherwise experienced, so here is where they are occasionally offered bits of cheese and chicken.

But I'm still fairly careful about the type of treat-food they are getting. Hence the kind of dialogue which is suffered by a poor assistant working in a service station on the journey north.

'Do you have any packets of chicken pieces?'

'Yes, just over there by the milk.'

'Ah . . . no, those are flame-grilled spicy ones, my dogs need the plain kind.'

At which point she will say firmly, 'Who's next please?', before watching the strange man leave and climb into his car, chatting to the occupants as he does so.

'Sorry, girls, no chicken there. We'll try the Waitrose at the next stop.'

And so, my rucksack is filled for these not at all spoiled dogs. And after a five-hour doze, Mabel is ready for her first proper mountain experience.

29. Mabel, Munros and Memories

The Drumochter Pass is impressive enough, but does not immediately strike you as the most beautiful corner of the Highlands. It is either experienced from inside a train or, more often, from one of the thousands of cars, vans or lorries thundering up and down the A9 – the main road carrying traffic north and south in Scotland. Not many people pause here, or stop to set off into the hills on either side, unless you are one of the growing band of Munro-baggers – those who aim to climb every mountain over 3,000 feet in Scotland.

Among that collective, most would probably think of themselves as lifetime baggers – approaching it as a task to be completed over decades and enjoying knocking off one or two every now and again when the opportunity arises. There are others for whom it is closer to a full-time occupation and who approach Munros with, let's say . . . a greater devotion.

To complete (or 'compleat', to give it its traditional spelling) the full round of all 282 is quite the achievement. So consider for a moment the effort of Steven Fallon – the all-time leading Munro-bagger who is currently ticking them off on his sixteenth lap and every night, no doubt, says a quiet prayer for his knees.

More pertinently, as far as this book is concerned, is the encounter the dogs and I had on one of the summits of An Teallach when we were there for dawn on the final day of 2019.

We were milling around on the second peak, Sgurr Fiona, when this rather slight figure appeared and Olive gave her a customary abusive mountain-greeting.

I made more polite chat with this fellow hillwalker and asked if she might take a photo of the three of us, with the dark and dog-forbidding ridge in the background. I returned the favour, taking some really quite poorly framed and possibly out-of-focus shots for her, thinking that it would be a memento of a special day and achievement.

'Have you done An Teallach before?' I asked, with a tone that wasn't supposed to but probably came across as 'My goodness, haven't you done well to get up here!'

'Yes, a couple of times,' she replied with, what I would discover later that night, was a decidedly flexible usage of 'a couple'. For it turns out that this was Hazel Strachan – the woman with the most Munros tucked away in her rucksack, closing in on her eleventh circuit. I knew of Hazel and her achievement, but had no idea that this was the legendary Munroist herself – otherwise I would have asked her more about it all and perhaps why she keeps on doing it. And Olive and Mabel might have been more respectful instead of harassing her as she ate a sandwich.

Anyway, I should say that I am not a fully-committed Munro-bagger. I've done a hundred or so, and with every one that goes in the book I do consider the objective a little more seriously – but there are many majestic peaks which fall just short of the entirely arbitrary 3,000 feet mark and a good few which are a fraction higher and could be said to be rather dull by comparison.

The four Munros which we were about to take on, lying just to the west of the Drumochter Pass, might be ungenerously put into that latter category. The general rule in Scotland is that the further west you go, the sharper the mountains become – quite often there they will rise all the way from sea-level to summit at a rather lung-hurting angle. Here we were still far enough east to be in the broad, rounded mountains which lift out of already high ground like folds in a rug. They can seem benign yet, in the snows of winter, they are totally transformed. And on this day, once I had unfurled myself from my crouched driving position of the last few hours (reminding me of another reason why I am not ticking off Munros every day), they looked stunning – covered in white, with smooth summits catching the low January sun.

Since we have mentioned Munro numbers, Olive is probably around the fifty mark now, with Mabel at about twenty, but here Dog Junior was getting ready for her first. As I was strapping on a load which I felt was considerable, but would have an elite Sherpa still whistling cheerily, she was bouncing around, hustling us along in eager anticipation of something, anything – she didn't know what, but it didn't really matter, because she was certain that it was going to be good.

She was also saying her hellos to the other human member of our expedition that day. Olive and I had already enjoyed a couple of years of climbing with a chap called Iain Cameron, whom I had initially got to know through social media. We had some mutual connections and seemed to share a lot of the same interests – the one which is his overwhelming passion was given away by his Twitter avatar, which was a giant snowflake. Nowadays that might suggest he espouses liberal values to the frustration of a right-wing mob, but he had it then because he is a chionophile – a lover of snow – and one of the few true experts on the study of how long snow lasts in any given year and where it might remain in the hills and mountains of the UK, deep into the summer months. Iain is also passionate about climbing mountains and had already marched round these four, but was prepared to repeat the effort as Labrador guide. Olive recognised him from previous hikes and so they caught up and chatted a bit about old times, including a macaroni pie she had once tried to take from him, as we set off.

Now, having written that, I feel I should explain, as some of you who are not of the Scottish persuasion might be thinking it was a mistake. *A macaroni pie?* Surely you don't mean a pie with macaroni in it? But yes, that's exactly what it is. It is essentially mac and cheese inside a round pie case without a lid and is available from plenty of Scottish bakeries. And don't judge us until you have tried it – during or after a day in the mountains it is a wonderful thing. In fact, no mountains have to be involved at all.

Olive was very possibly still full of pie-thoughts as we started out, but with room for only one thing at a time inside a Labrador head it was soon replaced by another pleasure.

The Pass of Drumochter sits at 1,500 feet, so there was no real wait to reach the snowline and for the excited dance of all the chionophiles to begin – Mabel leading the way in the ecstasy.

Not that she was unfamiliar with snow, as shortly before this expedition Caroline had joined Olive, Mabel and me for an attempt on Meall nan Tarmachan (the Hill of the Ptarmigans), a very accessible peak on the north side of Loch Tay, just about as close to the geographical heart of Scotland as you can get. That climb was aborted when the wind suddenly whipped up to about fifty miles an hour and Caroline was blown off her feet. Olive and Mabel, being rather lower to the ground, couldn't really see what all the fuss was about although momentarily questioned why one of their people had come down to join them. So it was time to turn around, but it did let Mabel experience proper snow for the first time and it made quite an impression.

You might think, therefore, that just a few weeks later Mabel might be rather blasé about encountering snow again. But this would be to ignore the fact that (a) she has the memory of a particularly absent-minded goldfish and (b) she gets excited about almost everything. So, hitting the snow once more sent her into raptures, racing around with her backside tucked in and her ears down. She kept bounding over to Olive to share the overwhelming awesomeness of what she was experiencing, but Olive was now one of the seasoned pros and seemed to engage with Mabel in much the same way that I had with Hazel Strachan. 'Oh, well done you . . . First time in the snow? Yes – great isn't it . . .'

And indeed, snow is great, although sinking into it with every step, as we were here, can make a climb rather arduous. But, in technical terms, these hills of Drumochter are simple, so we still made quick enough progress. Sometimes I wish I could experience the more dramatic mountains of Scotland with Olive and Mabel. They will never know the most exhilarating bits of An Teallach, or perhaps Liathach, or stand on top of the Cobbler, or experience the most dramatic of all – the awesome Cuillin of Skye – whose coarse granite would, in any case, be rather harsh on their paws.

That's not to say it's impossible for dogs to join in the scrambling fun. I did once meet a party of climbers on a particularly testing section on Bidean nam Bian in Glen Coe, who included in their number a Jack Russell. The solution to an obvious problem came about courtesy of the dog wearing a jacket which had a handle attached to the top, along his spine. He was thus picked up like a small piece of luggage and carried over the more technical parts of the route. Sometimes he was passed from one baggage-handler to another and it all looked fairly undignified, but he didn't seem to mind. And besides, while he was being passed around his little legs kept pumping away and in his head he no doubt felt that he was one of the world's foremost climbers. But, of course, this is only possible with lighter dogs and since neither Olive nor Mabel fit into this category we are restricted to less technical outings.

Still, on this January day, the Drumochter outing was offering more than its fair share of visceral pleasures. In particular, it seemed, for Mabel, who was experiencing this kind of thing for the first time. The sensation of bounding through deep snow, or being momentarily startled and then intrigued when that very snow came to life in a feathery white explosion as a squawking ptarmigan took flight. And it appeared to be most welcome when a pure white mountain hare set off at the approach of our wolves and both Olive and Mabel gave chase in lumbering pursuit, sinking into the snow as the hare bounced across the surface like a well-skimmed stone.

What's more, it all added to our own experience. Our human joy in the climb was multiplied by seeing the dogs taking such pleasure from it – chasing snowballs and generally frolicking and scampering around in the snow like fools. After all, isn't that exactly the same sort of pure and innocent fun we have all enjoyed at some point but is perhaps now largely forgotten in the busy lives we create for ourselves?

The fun, though, was checked for a moment as we approached our first summit, Sgairneach Mhòr, and Iain drew my attention to an enormous balcony of snow, overhanging the drop into the northern coire[4].

'Think it might be wise to get them on a lead.'

I couldn't have agreed more. Dogs have a great sense of heights and the danger that they pose. But what you can add, to the incredibly long list of things which they don't understand, is cornices.

I was reminded of a long day back in Torridon, soon after Olive appeared in our lives, climbing beautiful Slioch by Loch Maree with her and Caroline. I had stopped on the summit to take some photos as Caroline headed off down towards the ridge which led on to a subsidiary peak. Olive was by my side, but a moment later she was not. With her other human briefly lost from sight over a crest, she had felt it her solemn duty to gallop off and find her. Unfortunately, her galloping was in a slightly different direction and, to my dismay, she was now heading over to a sizeable cornice hanging over an equally sizeable drop. Of course, she did stop before what she thought was the edge, but now she was standing over space, supported only by insecure spring snow.

---

4. A coire, (or corrie) from the Gaelic word for 'pot', is the Scottish equivalent of what is known geographically as a 'cirque' – a feature of mountains whereby glacial erosion has scooped out a concave valley, open at one end and rising steeply at the head.

Well, I have never offered her so many biscuits/walks/hard cash in such a desperate and pleading tone. Thankfully she scampered back to me to make sure that I had put it all down in writing and I was most grateful that she was only about twenty-five kilos and the cornice had stood firm. Mungo would have plummeted through immediately and possibly still been rolling to this day.

Anyway, with leads on here we soon reached the first summit and congratulated Mabel on her debut Munro by staging a presentation of a small piece of chicken. She then made a speech that started well, but rather lost its way and became more about how she would like some additional food, before the music was faded up and she was escorted off the stage.

Indeed, on this day of firsts, it was here that 'Mountain Mabel' – a darker, more forceful version of our younger dog – made her initial appearance. Normally very polite and respectful of eating regulations, she clearly felt that different rules applied out in the wild, as if we were on a private yacht in international waters and could drink and gamble to our hearts' content. She was also very pleased to discover that her long snout was very handy for digging into the depths of the rucksack and seeing what else she might find.

They were enjoying their regular fuel-stops and we were savouring the views as we moved on to Beinn Udlamain, looking down on Loch Ericht and across to stately and enormous Ben Alder and then moved on to our third of the day, A' Mharconaich.

Both Olive and Mabel were fascinated by a couple of things as we made our further progress; firstly, that humans could move down the slopes off one peak by simply sitting down and sliding. Olive, in particular, loves this – running alongside and wagging furiously. Perhaps she thinks we are trying out her own patented move of vigorously trying to remove some awkwardly stuck grass and so is merely offering support. The other thing which struck both of them was encountering a couple of ski-tourers coming the other way. The dogs were first thoroughly perplexed by these things which appeared to be half human, half stick, and then further amazed as they slid off down the slopes, Mabel staring for some time with head cocked before deciding to see if the answer might lie in the bottom of my rucksack.

We made a brief detour to knock off Geal Charn, our fourth Munro of the day (perhaps I am a bagger after all), and paused for a few more snaps and videos. Indeed, it was an outing which was recorded in some detail – a good few of my favourite photos of Olive, Mabel and me in snowy mountain scenery come from this day, courtesy of the photographic talents of Iain.

But it was soon back down to the car, farewell to our photographer, and a return to the road, Mabel still coming to terms with it all. We stopped after an hour or so, whereupon the dogs expressed their deep displeasure at being woken, before reconsidering when I fed them in the car park of a pub in Pitlochry. Then we all trooped into this dog-friendly establishment so that they might be able to stare at me having my dinner, keeping the great Labrador hope alive that a pea or carrot, or perhaps an entire steak might somehow fall to the floor. Eventually they had to abandon that optimistic vigil as the warm room and the fatigue of the day took over – falling asleep in front of the fire to dream of hares and ptarmigans, high mountains and soft snow. And their noses twitched only briefly as another course arrived.

30. Dogs Welcome

Unlike in that Pitlochry pub, sometimes even man's – or woman's – best friend is not welcome. Once, signs declaring 'No Dogs' were to be found in many public places or businesses. Now much of our human world is starting to open up to the canine.

Shops are still pretty much a no-go area unless you have an assistance dog. Although one of my favourite stores for outdoor equipment does welcome them in – the same one where Olive decides that she can't cope with a slight change in the texture of the floor. In fact, Olive has a habit of letting herself down in this company's stores. Another branch which I frequent has a giant model sheep at the heart of its centrepiece display and on an early visit there she stood and barked at it so loudly and continuously that I felt deeply ashamed. 'It was awful,' I told Caroline later. 'To make up for it I had to buy all this equipment and unnecessary expensive clothing.'

Plenty of cafés do welcome dogs – although again, Olive tends to rule out the majority. She will trot in through the door and then apply the front-paw brakes, having taken against the floor. So I find myself shouting my order for a flat white from the doorway and asking if they could possibly bring the card machine over as Mabel, with no such flooring concerns, heads to the counter and selects a muffin.

Still, some people do not like dogs and I completely understand that – it certainly doesn't make them bad people. If you want a nice relaxing coffee and have a yapping or perhaps slightly grubby creature appear beside you then it can sully the experience. I feel this way about many children. Or you might be averse, or allergic, to dog fur. I would always ask people nearby if they minded me sitting there with our dogs and if they say yes then I'll try and find a seat somewhere else – if there isn't one available then I'll give an apologetic shrug and park myself beside them. Then offer an even bigger shrug and perhaps financial compensation as Olive knocks over their drinks to get at a proton-sized crumb beneath their table.

One of our favourite destinations is Altrincham Market in that town south-west of Manchester. It is one of the finest eating places for miles around – a foodies' heaven with lots of small businesses serving from stalls around the large, open eating area of the old indoor market, where tables seat about eight and people often end up sharing with others.

Crucially it also welcomes dogs. Well, as a whole it does,

'Tasting absolutely nothing.'

'I would rather stay in here
a bit longer, thanks.'

'Mabel sensing this might be a chance. Still waiting . . . still believing . . .'

Hard but fair management. Confronting Mabel about
Kevin the Dobermann from Accounts.

Looking out to Skye's Cuillin Ridge from Blà Bheinn.
Olive has spotted something edible two miles away.

Catch of the Day.

Panorama of Ben Alder ignored. Biscuits more important.

Olive above the clouds on Ben Lawers.

The best mountain companions.

Matching coats for the steep slopes of An Stùc. I think Mabel's cost more.

On the first peak of An Teallach – photo taken by Hazel Strachan. Telling Olive and Mabel they can have a snack if they try the ridge behind me.

Skis and spindrift on Chno Dearg.

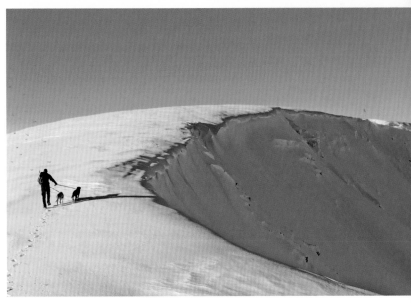

The importance of leads, with dogs' understanding of cornices limited.

Just occasionally in the mountains Mabel needs a bit of reassurance.

Wimbledon Centre Court. Working with John McEnroe, I look as concerned as Mabel.

The Olympic Opening Ceremony in Rio de Janeiro – 198 countries still to do.

Looking out from the crater's edge on Mount Fuji.

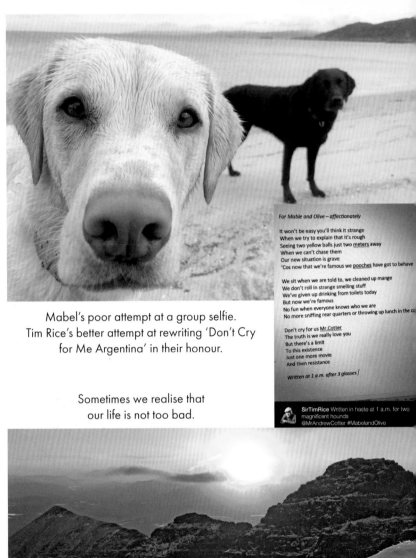

Mabel's poor attempt at a group selfie.
Tim Rice's better attempt at rewriting 'Don't Cry
for Me Argentina' in their honour.

For Mable and Olive – affectionately

It won't be easy you'll think it strange
When we try to explain that it's rough
Seeing two yellow balls just two meters away
When we can't chase them
Our new situation is grave
'Cos now that we're famous we pooches have got to behave

We sit when we are told to, we cleaned up mange
We don't roll in strange smelling stuff
We've given up drinking from toilets today
But now we're famous
No fun when everyone knows who we are
No more sniffing rear quarters or throwing up lunch in the ca

Don't cry for us Mr.Cotter
The truth is we really love you
But there's a limit
To this existence
Just one more movie
And then resistance

Written at 1 a.m. after 3 glasses |

SirTimRice Written in haste at 1 a.m. for two
magnificent hounds
@MrAndrewCotter #MabelandOlive

Sometimes we realise that
our life is not too bad.

although you can see clearly who the non-dog fans are as you walk in. In fact you can read about it on the wall as, in a very British, self-deprecating way, they write out and stick up little cards with any bad reviews from Trip Advisor – thrown onto the internet in indignation by those who have visited and were disappointed that this wonderful place of the highest-quality food from caring, independent traders was not quite the KFC they were looking for. The fact that there might also be dogs is enough to drive some to the keyboard.

'So unhygienic to allow dogs. I will NOT be back' is a typical complaint, bashed out in impotent rage and the hope that this one-person protest will bring a thriving business to its knees.

But I am not oblivious or unfeeling about the wishes of non-dog people at all. This is why I really do try to make a subtle, dignified entry and quietly take our seats. It's just that Olive and Mabel do not do subtle when entering any new place, instead crashing through the doors shouting 'GREETINGS, one and all! Let's get this party STARTED . . .' Even with harnesses on I cut quite a figure, leaning back at forty-five degrees to act as a counterweight to the dogs, who are pulling as if reaching the crucial stages in a Yukon sledge race. Throughout it all, while straining every sinew, I try and maintain a casual and breezy manner to give the impression that I am in total control and that nobody should be in the least bit concerned about the rabid wolves who have just entered the dining area.

Eventually we settle down – the chances are that a lot of space has magically opened up around us – and Olive begins her very important work of getting her lead tangled around as many chair legs as possible. Then she invites herself to nearby gatherings, just to say hello, check-in and wonder if they might have any nibbles going spare.

By her normal barometer this floor surface should dissuade her, but she graciously makes an exception for it because it has a tendency to harbour crumbs and micro-morsels of food between the boards.

Those working there seem to love the dogs and will often bring across a bowl of water. This very much piques their interest, but as it is lowered to the floor in front of them you can almost see the disappointment spreading across Olive's face.

'Ah, sorry, I actually ordered one of the bacon ciabattas . . .'

Mabel will drink because she's both very polite and easily led but she is also – quite frankly – terrible at it, with her technique a model of inefficiency. At the very most about ten per cent of the water which leaves the bowl will make it into her mouth, the rest being splashed around a wide radius so that by the time she is done anywhere on the floor within five feet is soaking and now flouting health and safety guidelines. The poor person who brought the water bowl in the first place is beginning to regret their generosity as they head off to get a mop. Others are reaching for their phones and downloading the Trip Advisor app.

But it is in going away on a break that the 'dogs welcome' rule becomes even more relevant. You might find the most beautiful cottage in the Highlands, which ticks every box except for the most important one – no dogs. Again, I understand that entirely. There are plenty of folk who will not want to be staying in a place where dogs have been.

There's a website I often visit which usefully, but very starkly, lays it out in their accommodation pages. I could really hurt my dogs' feelings by telling them that they seem to be an afterthought, below the list of available amenities, just after a symbol letting us know if the place has a washing machine or Wi-Fi. If hounds are allowed there is a little black dog icon, which looks as if it could have been modelled on Olive. Or if they don't, the Olive lookalike has a red line through it, as if taken out by a sniper. And given the bluntness of some of the Bed & Breakfast owners I have spoken to on the phone, it's a distinct possibility.

Yet sometimes you can be taken by surprise at the grand and luxurious lodgings which will accept four-pawed guests. I was once invited to speak at a function at Gleneagles, one of Scotland's most famous and venerable hotels, set in rolling Perthshire countryside, and had been told initially that dogs were allowed but had to stay in the kennels on site.

Well, let me make it quite clear – compared to those dogs who might sleep outside, or work, or hunt, Olive and Mabel have enjoyed a soft and pampered life. They would arrive at the kennels and ask if they might have their bags brought up, while the other hardened inmates rattled their bowls on the bars and jeered 'Fresh meat . . .' as our two walked past the cells.

But fortunately for Olive (as it was only her then) my information had been incorrect. Not only were dogs welcome in the hotel itself, but they were provided with their own towel, bowls and biscuits – as well as a little sign to hang outside on the door handle, telling anyone who might drop by that there was a dog inside. As it happens, no sign was necessary, since any footsteps which padded past our door triggered Olive into believing that there were intruders inside her enormous new house. In particular, one gentle inquiry of 'Housekeeping?' was met with such a volley of abuse that we forfeited our right to a turn-down service for the rest of our stay.

Gleneagles was also where we discovered that Olive is not a supporter of lifts – particularly if they contain mirrored walls or, as she chose to see it, several other dogs. The unpleasantness of the situation was heightened as the lift began its ascent and Olive went to her default safe-mode of spreading herself as low as possible. She was at least consoled to see that all of the other dogs in there were finding it equally traumatic.

I don't wish to give the impression that our dogs are in any way spoiled but once, as a rare treat on the way back from a mountain expedition, I decided to stop in at another high-end establishment. The Cromlix is a fairly new hotel, but has been created from a converted Victorian mansion and is already very well-known because its owner is Andy Murray – arguably Scotland's greatest sporting star – who is from the nearby town of Dunblane.

The good news for Olive and Mabel is that, perhaps because Andy is a dog lover and also no doubt because the hotel is used by some folk as a base for shooting expeditions (again, I'm frowning), it does accept dogs with open arms. Of course, you might say that for the cost involved you should be able to turn up with five or six bison if desired, but actually it was quite reasonable when I was there out of season and all the staff made a goodly fuss of the two lively and hirsute guests. Those same guests then dragged me through the very pleasant library/lounge area where couples in their evening finery sipped cocktails and aperitifs, with Olive insisting on mingling and wondering if there might be an amuse-bouche or two going spare.

Unable to leave them alone, I was restricted to a room-service dinner, with both dogs agreeing that this was *quite* the most brilliant thing in the world that food should simply appear – but only after the poor member of staff who had knocked on the door was forced to hear what Olive thought about his mother. The charms of the enormous bathroom with heated floor were rather lost on her very selective paws, but overall both decided that they had greatly enjoyed this place, as I made them even softer and less-suited to any future kennel experience. Incidentally, the fact that I had taken our dogs for a night away to this luxurious hotel without Caroline was not entirely appreciated. I think I tried to keep it a secret before Olive told her all about it when we got back home.

Again, perhaps I am giving something of the wrong impression – as if Olive and Mabel are pampered individuals who enjoy a nice spa weekend here and there. And they very possibly do. But more often they are being put through their paces by me – their leader and sometime master. A drill sergeant who is *desperately* trying to keep the regiment together as they go through their exercises.

31. Run With Us

It's a great shame that dogs have so far failed to master cycling.

I say this because it would mean another activity which I could do with Olive and Mabel. You see, I'm at that age where men, in particular, have a tendency to slip into Lycra now and again – at just that time of life when a body can become entirely unsuited to such material. But, due to my own poor hip-score, cycling is something of a necessity if you don't want to be pounding your joints on a run.

Who knows, perhaps it could work with my dogs. I can see Mabel on a sit-up-and-beg bicycle (naturally), little bows on the handlebars and a basket on the front, into which she could put all of her pointless but deeply treasured things. Meanwhile I'd be riding a tandem with Olive, thinking it was a bit of a struggle before turning round to see her, feet up, reading a magazine.

Thankfully, none of this nonsense has come to pass, since I can still manage a run or two with them and it is – behind eating, sleeping and swimming – one of their very favourite things to do.

Again, for them it must be something to do with the pack mentality – a deeply buried remnant of pre-domesticated days when the wolves ran to hunt or to escape. Although I have to say that our running pack is not entirely cohesive.

Mabel is a fully paid-up member and will stick beside me for the full distance. It's very useful because I know exactly where she is, although occasionally frustrating as I trip over her. I get the impression that she also wonders why we are all running and has concerns that we might be in some dreadful peril. Are we being chased by a lion?

Every now and again she looks up at me for reassurance, or casts a worried glance behind, checking to see if we have managed to shake off our imaginary pursuers. Then she will notice a squirrel up ahead and produce a ferocious burst of speed, before the squirrel darts up into the sanctuary of a tree and Mabel wonders what dark magic has caused it to disappear.

Olive seems to have subscribed only to off-peak membership of the pack. She runs to a different rhythm, which can be hugely irritating – a couple of hundred yards with us, then she'll go off to do her own thing. Usually she catches up with bits of foliage attached, hinting at great adventures, but sometimes she doesn't reappear at all. After a mile or so without her Mabel starts to look concerned, certain in her head that the lion has finally got one of us, so I turn back. The reason is usually far simpler – either Olive has stopped by people who have food and consequently no power on earth can shift her, or she has wandered into the trees where some unfortunate creature has expired. I'll find her, upside down in the cadaver, tongue hanging out and legs waving in the air, as if to say, 'It's what he would have wanted.'

The most aggravating part of it all is that if I ever run with somebody else – my friend Tom, for example – Olive will stick by his side the whole way, never disappearing or even dropping her pace. On these occasions I'm surprised that I can run through the tears.

On very rare occasions when they have both been distracted and wandered off, I try to hide to teach them a lesson – again, an example of how inadequate and misguided my training methods are. My slightly confused thinking is that my sudden disappearance from their lives will cause them such great angst that they will immediately drop everything to try and find me. Whereas the reality is that they simply enjoy the peace and quiet, left alone to carry on eating or rolling uninterrupted. So there I am, crouching down behind a tree, waiting and waiting until a good few minutes have gone. Eventually a couple of respectable-looking women are the first to pass by and are understandably startled by this sweaty, heavily breathing figure lurking in the undergrowth.

'It's fine. I'm just waiting for those two behind you,' I say, as if this explanation will somehow make things better. Then, five minutes later and with an approaching police siren, I give up and decide that I should go back to find my dogs and get my story straight.

Again, though, as in the mountains, I am aware that I am responsible for them – they will try and run all day if asked (well, Mabel would) but you have to take care. Running with them in the summer is not really an option – I mean, you try it in a coat that can keep you warm up a mountain at minus fifteen.

But, as previously discussed, they are both slender dogs – from working lines. Labradors have the reputation for being on the chunky side and, indeed, a show Labrador might well be able to do a bit of sprinting or lumber along for a while, but six-mile jogs would not necessarily be their thing. Mabel, though, will give most dogs a good run for pace. She once chased a greyhound in wide-ranging loops for about ten minutes, utterly convinced that she was going to catch it, with the greyhound jogging along just out of reach, casually smoking a cigarette.

As all runners know, however, it is a pastime which does come with the risk of injury – and before Mabel was part of the run club it did lead to Olive requiring a trip to the vee-ee-tee.

The problem didn't come from the run itself, but from when she leaped out of the boot of the car with the usual enthusiasm of a dog at that stage in proceedings. In doing so, she caught a paw on a metal catch and a claw was torn off. Blood fairly pouring out, she hopped around a bit and in the game fashion of dogs was still suggesting that she could just run it off – it's really nothing, no more than a scratch, please ignore this gathering red pool around my paw and can we get going? Then I had to break the bad news that, as well as the run now not happening, we would also be making a visit to the place where all dogs fear to go.

A few hours later, the paw was bandaged and Olive's day was not proceeding as advertised. Her eyes had attained that level of looking sorry for oneself that only dogs can achieve, accompanied by constant sighing exhalations. It also meant a return to the cone of shame and, in addition, on any subsequent outings we had to cover her paw in a plastic sandwich bag. There was really not much more we could do to add insult to her injury. It was akin to those internet videos where people put more and more stuff on their docile and accepting pets for entertainment and I momentarily thought about fetching a book, or a shoe, or perhaps a toaster and piling it all on – but she had suffered enough.

Anyway, Olive wore bandage, bag and cone with great sadness and humiliation for a month or so, until the claw, like a fingernail, had simply grown back and we were soon jogging the trails once again.

Which was good news, as not only is it fun, but it's also essential training for both our dogs. Because occasionally, I do rather test their stamina to the limits.

32. The Incredible Journey

The alarm sounds at 4.30 a.m.

There, you see . . . I do still have to set it sometimes. For when I decide I need to get up even earlier than my dogs desire.

How much you come to hate that sound – it doesn't matter which one you choose on your phone for the task. However pleasant or soothing or perky it may be, you hate it as if the devil himself has composed the electronic jingle. It's like having Kenny G at the end of the bed going through his back catalogue.

It's even harder to rouse myself now, with the night still pitch black. In fact, there won't be light for another four hours and at this time of year the days barely get fully light at all.

I can just make out the shape of Mabel, raising a head with crumpled ears from the rug on the bed to see *what on earth* is going on at this hour. She's supposed to be in her own bed on the floor in this rented cottage, but her neediness in the small hours often gets the better of her – in particular if we are somewhere strange and she decides that she just has to be lying against something familiar. I can't see Olive at all as she disappears in the darkness – but I know she won't have moved, valuing her sleep too much. And, bearing in mind what this day has in store, she is wise to grab every possible moment.

I haven't slept too well either. Firstly, because both dogs seem to have been involved in the latter stages of a snoring contest and, secondly, because this cottage, lovely though it is, sits right beside the main railway line – the same one that cuts through the Drumochter Pass further south. The name 'Railway Cottage' should have given me a clue, as every now and then a train thunders past a few feet away and the windows shake. The other reason is that when I know I have to get up early, even with an alarm set, I will wake up every half hour or so to make sure that I am awake in time for my alarm.

Only two things can motivate me to make such an early start – either a flight somewhere, when the initial feeling is quickly replaced by one of dread at the prospect of taxis, airports and planes. Or because I am heading for the mountains, in which case the early sluggishness gives way to nervous excitement at the day ahead. And this is going to be a long day. Although I've managed to choose one of the shortest of the year, a couple of weeks into December, to take on the biggest mountain expedition I've attempted – a round of four of the highest peaks in Scotland, twenty-five miles in total. Eight thousand feet of climbing. In the snow.

Yes, this may seem rather ambitious, but in a Scottish winter the windows of decent weather and good snow conditions are only rarely open. So when you get a chance you take it and, because I have to make a fair old journey to get there, I like to make the most of it when I do, cramming in as much distance and as many peaks as I can.

So that's why I find myself here, stumbling around by the feeble light of a bedside lamp and knowing that it's all going to be worth it. Neither Olive nor Mabel have the motivation of that knowledge, so they decide it's too early for such nonsense and curl themselves up into even tighter balls.

I am alone in the kitchen, pouring myself a cup of ambition. The dogs are still sleeping and won't move unless . . . I rummage for only a second or two in their food bag. Then turn around and there they are, sitting perfectly, bright-eyed and eager, like rounding a corner and being surprised by the twins of *The Shining*. They may be thinking that it's quite early to be having breakfast, but they're prepared to roll with it. Food overrides all other Labrador desires.

Half an hour later we are on the road to our start point for the day, the Sugar Bowl car park on the road out of Aviemore, on the way up to the Cairngorm ski centre. It is a very artificial base camp for what will be a long day getting away from man-made things.

There aren't many areas of wilderness left in the UK, but parts of the Cairngorms National Park feel as close as any. Further north in Scotland you might find more desolate areas of genuine wild, whereas here you do have the road and the ski-lifts, and 1960s-styled Aviemore is never too far away, but once you head further in towards the great rounded whaleback mountains, you very quickly leave all civilisation behind. In the winter, the high ground there – on a plateau where you can walk for miles without dropping below three thousand feet – is similar in look and feel to an arctic tundra.

On the twenty-minute drive Olive and Mabel have recommenced full sleep mode and don't look too enamoured with the prospect of leaving their warm beds when I open the boot. They know this routine and will be starting to suspect that their morning stroll may be further than to the end of the lane and back.

It is bitterly cold and oh-so-dark as I flit around, getting ready, with my head torch lighting up the night air and puffs of warm breath that rise and disappear like smoke. Boots on, gaiters on and check once again that everything required for this day of days is in the rucksack. Crampons, ice axe, poles, gloves, hand-warmers, first-aid kit, mobile phone chargers and spare clothing for all concerned. And enough food and water to feed three hungry bodies over the next twelve hours. Hat on, collars on and away we go – wondering briefly if I should make Olive and Mabel carry some stuff.

All they are carrying are lights on their collars. Otherwise Olive would simply sink into the blackness again, only resurfacing as two floating bright eyes caught in the beam of my torch. Mabel would be far less effective as a night-time assassin with her light fur easily illuminated and even picked up by the glow of the moon above.

'Pace yourself. A long way to go,' I say constantly and pointlessly to the dogs. In particular Mabel, who bounces around on the icy path and into the heather. 'Hey . . . Take it easy,' – but she is away, wasting her energy like the fun runner in a marathon making a mad sprint at the start just to get on TV.

Anyway, they're enjoying it and I'm in my element as well – never happier than in the pitch black, leading these two on somewhere. Unfortunately, I also know the barrier of the Chalamain Gap is coming. From our starting point it is the key to the whole day, as it lets us come in from our side-avenue, opening up the great cleft of the Lairig Ghru, the pass which cuts north to south between, among others, the huge lumps of Ben Macdui and Braeriach, the second and third highest mountains in the country.

Everything beyond will be down to simple fitness and determination, but none of that will matter if we can't get past the technicalities of the Gap. It's a very narrow col between surrounding hills which closes into a pinch point where hundreds of boulders have fallen down the slopes on either side, creating a jumble of rocks of all sizes at the base, and the only way to get through is to clamber over them.

Just to be clear, none of it is a problem to a human. A little bit of confidence and you could bounce through in ten minutes. In the dark with a glaze of ice perhaps fifteen. Throw in a couple of dogs and it's an entirely different matter.

It is also a decidedly eerie place which makes it all the more forbidding. And in the dark and the total stillness, without another soul around, the otherworldliness of it is beautiful and slightly unsettling. If a silence can echo, it does there and the few sounds which do escape are magnified. Every heavy breath, or the clink of an ice axe as it catches the edge of a rock. Or the scratch of claws on stone and whimpers of those who are not entirely happy with the turn this walk has taken.

Generally in life Olive is steadier of temperament and more relaxed, but here she is the first to express misgivings. It must go back to her lack of trust in certain floors or ground conditions. So, faced with one gap between boulders, on go the brakes with a bit of a shiver and a pleading face. It is quite enough to melt my heart and my overwhelming instinct is to protect them. I know there's absolutely no danger at all, but they don't. So, with soothing words, I go through the following procedure:

1. Pick Dog A up and carry over the perceived difficulty. Place down with an encouraging tone and more words to suggest that it was a bit of fuss over nothing. Administer biscuit.

2. Return to Dog B who has now joined in to register her disapproval at the situation. Repeat process.

Do this about twenty times with wriggling and anxious dogs each weighing twenty-five kilos and the four hundred metres of the Chalamain Gap has taken about three-quarters of an hour to get across. But we've made it, just as the very first hints of daylight are threatening the darkness and the long climb begins – or it does once Mabel has had another moment or two of snow-inspired madness where she bounds around like a loon with news of exciting developments under her paws. Once more I am worried that she is burning a lot of energy early in the day, but she doesn't immediately share my concerns.

We need all the reserves we have – Braeriach is huge. Approaching from the north the haul up the shoulder of Sròn na Lairige ('Nose of the Pass') involves no technicality but it just goes on and on, only after an hour or so the gradient easing as you reach something of a plateau. But this is where your mind is playing cruel tricks, because the summit of Braeriach itself is still a long slog away. And on this exposed plateau the wind has started to blow hard, so on go Finland's finest, and possibly most overpriced, dog coats.

I think it is the strangeness of the environment, the noise of the wind or the lack of visibility which gets to Mabel more than the temperature. I take encouragement that Olive in these situations is almost always entirely calm – which makes her inability to ride on a ferry, or walk into any number of cafés, even more ridiculous.

Eventually we reach the lip on the edge of Coire Brochain. 'Brochain' meaning porridge, which was supposed to be the consistency of any poor sheep or cattle found at the bottom, who had absent-mindedly wandered in the wrong direction in centuries past. And since absent-mindedness is a particular talent of Olive and Mabel, I take great care as we approach the sculptures of snow, blown up in artistic waves to cornices on the edge. I keep them at least ten feet away from the drop as I make them pose for photos to get some likes on Instagram.

The good news is that the wispy cloud around us is clearing fast and the views are glorious as we reach the summit of Braeriach – a pale December sun now doing the best it can. Only Ben Macdui, just across the pass, and Ben Nevis itself are higher points in the land. It means that there is not much more climbing for a while on the broad, flat, high ground as we skirt round the corries to our left and a safe distance away. Olive and Mabel are now having a grand old time, the coats have been removed and they trot around on the surface of the wind-scoured snow while their heavier human sinks through the crust with almost every step. I am reminded again that I should really try ski-touring.

Still, we make the next Munro, Sgòr an Lochain Uaine (fifth highest in the country if you're keeping a record) and then on to Cairn Toul (fourth on the list) and here Olive suddenly stiffens, before launching herself down the mountainside at a couple of dots in the distance. Mabel stands beside me, huffing and puffing and setting hackles to max, hoping that her friend can sort things out and that she doesn't have to get involved.

For the next minute or so I am looking on, as if watching a radar screen, with those two tiny, stationary dots bracing for a single dot incoming at speed.

But it's friendly fire and, as all the dots meet, they seem to be getting on famously. Eventually Mabel and I reach the dot-people – two brothers from Northern Ireland who have stayed overnight in the Corrour bothy (a basic mountain hut) down in the Lairig Ghru after climbing Ben Macdui the day before. But they seem to be as comfortable with extended conversation as I am.

'Some day . . .'

'Aye it is. Some day . . .'

'Have a good one.'

After thus putting the world to rights, Olive graciously lets them continue on their way and we now have to try and pick up the pace, as it's all taking rather longer than I would have liked. It's already one o'clock and at this time of year that means only about three hours of daylight remaining. That, though, becomes only a secondary concern as I notice a trail of red spots in the snow, and my heart sinks as I follow that trail to Olive.

Perhaps she did it in her vigorous guard-dog sprint down the mountain, but the injury is quickly traced to one of her dewclaws. These are the claws which are higher up on the side of a dog's leg, set apart from the rest of the claw family – they seem to be equivalents of our thumbs in location, but without all the useful talents of those human digits. I am told that dewclaws, even in their higher position, can help dogs with traction when sprinting, but day to day it seems that their main purpose is to get caught on things. I'm sure that's what happened here – the edge of a rock or a crampon or a walking pole. Perhaps she has even done it herself, attempting to chew off her own paw so that I call mountain rescue and she can be airlifted out of here. But the cause doesn't really concern me now – all that matters is that the ingeniously heated dog-paw blood is dripping out on to the snow.

So, first things first – we have to forget about the Penis of the Demon. I'm sorry if you've just spilled your tea, but that is what our fourth Munro of the day is called. Or *was* called – 'Bod an Deamhain' to be precise. That is until John Brown, the famous ghillie of Queen Victoria, gave it a censor-friendly name, 'the Devil's Point', to spare her blushes (it really was a priggish time). Return it to the original I say, and leave it in the Gaelic if you must, as few will understand it, let alone come over all unnecessary at the mere mention of a demonic appendage.

Right now, though, I'm more worried about the Paw of the Dog. It might be frustrating to have to leave out a very simple peak, but it's an easy decision to make. Olive is depositing regular spots of red in the snow and I'm starting to weigh up our options. It couldn't have happened in a more isolated place, with the nearest vet in Aviemore and our car still about eight hours' walk away. I also wonder if I'm going to have to carry her – clearing out my rucksack and putting her in, like a child in a papoose.

The thing is, she does seem to be walking on it fine. But in my mind I'm conjuring up the worst-case scenario – starting to worry that she'll lose enough blood to make her faint, in the manner of a nineteenth-century monarch on being told that some nearby hills look rather like a pair of tits.

But, as with a lot of dog injuries and illnesses, it was all an over-reaction from an overprotective owner. It had really been no more than us getting a cut around a fingernail. By the time we reach Corrour bothy and I get out the first-aid kit I see that my poor bandaging skills are not going to be necessary, as the cold of the snow seems to have performed some sort of cauterising miracle and the flow of blood has all but stopped.

So now I look back longingly at the Devil's Protuberance,

high above us, and think of what we have missed out on. But, in all honesty, it's not that impressive (perhaps that's why he was so angry all the time), and we're not heading back up there. Getting out of here is the only priority and there's still a long way to go and not much light remaining.

This is also where my concern for my dogs starts to take effect. You see, we're fine. Yes, I'm exceedingly tired, but humans are designed to walk or jog all day – it's how we used to catch our dinner before the drive-thru McDonald's came along. Early man on the plains of Africa could trot along for hours behind a poor creature who was meant for shorter, faster bursts of speed and then wait for it to tire, before lobbing a rock at it. I may be sketchy on some of the finer details, but essentially long distances are not a problem for modern homo sapiens, as long as your lifestyle doesn't involve picking up all of your food from a window while sitting in a car.

Members of Canis familiaris are also capable of running for a long time – remember their ancestors hunting in packs – but they still have their limits and you can quite clearly tell where they draw the line as they will simply decide to take a rest. After three miles of further effort down the Lairig Ghru (which is not flat, but rises slowly and cruelly to its highest point), I have to stop for the occasional snack to lift depleted energy levels. Yet, even with food nearby, both Olive and Mabel feel that their priority is to take this chance for a snooze, diligently digging out holes in the snow and then curling up after first turning round and round. Then round and round some more, until they are completely satisfied with the precise number of rotations they have completed, before asking if I might turn the light out and bring them a biscuit and possibly a glass of milk.

Sadly, I have to extricate them from their beds and chivvy them along, because the light is turning out without my help. I'm now worried that they are going full Jarvis on me and might just raise a weary paw, saying 'Carry on without me. Send help . . .', but thankfully they get up and we troop on – the remaining miles are going to be a test of endurance in the dark. But they are also hypnotic and beautiful. The night sky is clear and, if I switch off my head torch, seen from a place of total blackness free of man-made light, it is wondrous – millions of stars flickering above us. Even with the fatigue and the need to keep moving, I take a chance to sit down with the dogs and bring them in close. I look up and try to identify the constellations while chatting away to them: 'I think that might be Venus . . . and over there . . . yes! . . . I'm sure that's Sirius, the Dog Star,' which certainly seems to get their attention until I realise that it's actually a plane and both Olive and Mabel start digging burrows again.

Route-finding is not easy with the path under the cover of snow, but there is a burden of responsibility. Every time I turn round I see four eyes in the dark close behind – Olive and Mabel are tired and in their faithful and misguided heads I'm their wise leader.

'Of *course* he knows what he's doing – stick with him and we'll be fine.'

'Okay. He just . . . seems to be swearing quite a lot.'

But after an hour or two or possibly three, we have found our way back to the Chalamain Gap. It is just as eerie in the dark of the evening as it was in the morning, a long, long expedition ago – possibly even more difficult now with my tired limbs, but the advantage is that dog fatigue seems to be acting as a mild sedative and there are fewer complaints heading in this direction. Safely through, the last stretch back to the car park is on a more distinct path and it should be easy enough from here. Although, with one slight drop down to cross a burn and climb back up the other side, even I am considering the option of digging a hole, circling round a few times and curling up in a ball.

'Nearly there . . .' I keep saying in encouraging tones to the dogs, but as much for my own benefit. And besides, they've long since stopped listening. Even Mabel has lost her joie de vivre, ignoring the heather into which she bounded twelve hours ago. Olive's chin is nearly scraping along the ground and she looks to be considering how she can stretch her cut paw into a near-death experience when telling Caroline.

But finally, a twenty-five-mile round trip behind us, we are back at the car and with a groan of relief I remove the rucksack. I won't even ask the dogs to jump into the boot, rather I use my own last reserves of energy to lift them up and they are asleep almost as I place them gently in their beds. I stroke their heads as eyes close and they drift away to the sound of me telling them they are the best dogs.

A short while later we are back at the cottage and, just before we all manage to eat our own bodyweight in food, I call Caroline to let her know that everyone has returned safely.

'How was it?'

'Long,' I reply. 'But, also I think . . . one of the greatest days of my life.'

No trains will rouse us tonight – the express from Glasgow could crash through the cottage itself and we would slumber on. I expect the dogs to now sleep for a couple of days straight – or at least Olive will, already twitching and snoring in front of the log-burner.

Yet as I go to lock up, there is a small nudge from a nose at the back of my knee. It's Mabel and she is risen . . . Just a little bit groggy and with one ear folded over, but firmly drawing my attention to the *two* walks a day which are in her contract thank you very much and requesting that we head out, no matter how impressive that first outing might have been.

'Come on then,' I say, as we set off on another great adventure of a loop around the garden.

33. Don't Leave Me This Way

One of the very few downsides of the job I do is the amount of travel involved. 'Oh . . . my poor thing. How *do* you cope with it?' And yes, I agree that it may not seem a hardship, getting paid to see the world and watch sport. But ignoring for a moment the fact that, for most of 2020 neither of those things was part of my life, I would like to disabuse you of any notion that travel is fun.

True, being in that foreign place is great – I've always appreciated the change of scenery and the very different environments and cultures. One of the most famous sayings of the great rugby commentator Bill McLaren was that a day out of Hawick was a day wasted – he would always make sure that he was back in his beloved town in the Scottish Borders by the night after the match, racing home from Paris, Dublin or Cardiff or London. I am not quite at that level – I can quite happily settle into a new place and a new routine, but still there are many things I miss about home.

One of them, of course, or rather two of them, are Olive and Mabel. In somewhat sad fashion when I'm away I will sit and scroll through videos of them on my phone. I'm always wary of somebody in the seat next to me on a plane, glancing over to see what film I'm watching and catching Mabel's enormous snout filling the screen.

'It's a Wes Anderson. Bit quirky . . .' I'll say by way of explanation.

Similarly, long before their famous Zoom call, I often tried to have chats with them on FaceTime but, foolish beasts that they are, they never connect the voice coming from this piece of metal and glass with the human they know. They usually end up having a scratch or just wandering off to do something more interesting, and I am left shouting their name, urging them to come back in a rather needy, high-pitched voice in a hotel room in Dubai.

There is, though, one great upside to being away from them (apart from being able to sleep past six a.m.), and that is the welcome I receive when I return. Towards the end of long tours it is never far from my thoughts and in the last few minutes of the journey back from the airport or driving down the motorway I am hitting the heights of anticipation reached by Mabel on a trip to the beach.

And it never disappoints. At the click of the latch on the gate there comes the sound of frantically scuttling claws from within the house. As I open the door there is always just a brief moment for full recognition to ignite in the dog brain (with Mabel always visibly a second or two behind) and then it begins. Olive is also slightly more together in greeting me with a specially selected toy – I'm sure that Mabel means to, but forgets amidst all the excitement and then tries to appropriate whatever Olive is carrying, taking on the role of someone at a party who's neglected to bring a present and subsequently claims that the nice gift which the hosts are opening 'is really from all of us'.

Then I sit down and they both start doing circles of the rug, wagging their entire bodies and making their respective noises – Olive with one repetitive bass growl of contentment, Mabel more high-pitched and featuring perhaps two or three notes. Together they sound as if they have got the band back together while I've been away and they're trying out their new material.

It is a wonderful thing to behold and makes all the days and weeks away worth it. Even if it is pretty much the same when I've been on a twenty-minute trip to the local supermarket.

Anyway, occasionally I do have surrogate dogs on my travels to help me through the time away. In Australia, with near-yearly trips to visit Caroline's brother Johnny and his family in Melbourne, we would always make good use of their two dogs, Charlie and Ralph – Charlie a flat-coated Retriever and Ralph a beast of many breeds.

In 2011 I stayed on after our holiday to cover the Australian Open tennis. Following the late-night sessions I would return to the house about one a.m. and Charlie (this was in pre-Ralph days) would be there to greet me and we'd sit together for a while in the warm Melbourne night air. Charlie with the gentle eyes and that open-mouthed slight panting that gave the impression of a cheery character who would chuckle away to himself at absolutely nothing or laugh very politely at all of your jokes.

'*Very* nice to see you again, sir . . . How did Andy Murray get on tonight, sir?'

'Yup, all good Charlie – he won in straight sets. Through to play Djokovic. No worry for Murray!'

'Ha-ha . . . Oh *good* one, sir! And that IS great news, fingers crossed for the final . . . Sleep well, sir.'

But it didn't matter where I might be in the world, I would always be happy to find a dog. No language skills are required and nothing is lost in translation – there is no cultural boundary to overcome. Wherever we may be, in whatever country, dogs will simply treat you as dogs always do – show them a bit of kindness and love and they will gladly return those sentiments. There's probably a lesson for all of us there.

Sometimes, for just a brief moment or two, I ponder how nice it would be to be able to have Olive and Mabel with us overseas. I consider how life (in particular a dog's) is too short to be away from them for weeks at a time, but then I snap back into reality and swiftly remove myself from one of the stupidest ideas I could have. I recognise the prospective awfulness for all parties concerned – the paperwork and procedures to endure, putting them through the stress of travelling in crates in the hold and the quarantine at the other end. For what? So that Olive could wilt in the heat and Mabel could fail to understand all manner of exotic creatures which she would put into her bulging internal folder marked 'Unknown'.

Instead, if both Caroline and I are away we rely on various options for dog accommodation. It used to be that a professional dog-walker called Dee would take them in and have them stay at her own house. Olive frequently tells us that the greatest Christmas she ever spent was when Caroline and I went to Australia and she was allowed to enjoy sofas and biscuits and roaring fires which apparently were so *very* much better than ours.

I am reminded of this whenever we are out on a walk and Olive shoots off into the distance because she has realised that Dee is somewhere within half a mile or so. We'll find her sitting adoringly at her feet and so we join up for the rest of the walk with Olive glued to her side. Mabel never really had the extended stays at Dee's house so doesn't have quite the same connection, although she does consider her perfectly pleasant company. Come the end of the walk, Olive will leap swiftly and decisively into the back of Dee's car, saying, 'Let's go – ditch these losers. I've made my choice,' and my heart breaks.

Now that Dee no longer takes boarders (we are assured that Olive wasn't the reason behind the decision), we rely on kennels, or 'Dog Hotels' as they are often grandly titled – no doubt to make owners feel a bit better about the whole thing. It's certainly easier on the conscience to head off to the airport imagining that beloved pets are somewhere glitzy and carpeted with an attached health club and spa, rather than a shed in a field.

In fact, the one frequented by Olive and Mabel really is very nice indeed and the people who work there hugely professional with an obvious love for dogs. Yet still they can rely on people like us and our overwhelming guilt so that, by the time we have added on the extras, we will end up spending more on the dogs' stay than we do on our own holiday. The sales pitch given to us on first contact with the kennels was the easiest they have ever had to make.

'Would you like a Standard or Executive room?'

'What's the difference?'

'Well, the Executives have a television in the corner that plays soothing music which calms anxious dogs. And that's been proven by actual *science*. They also get proper beds for the dogs to lie on rather than just dog beds in the corner. Of course, this makes no sense, but I'm guessing you'll do anything for them at this moment. And for a little bit more they can have a bespoke gift bag of a lavender and chamomile biscuit selection which they won't appreciate because . . . well, again, they're dogs. But did I mention that these rooms are only for very special *executive* dogs? Perfect . . . If you could just read the long number on the front of the card for me . . .'

Just occasionally we have gone for neither of the boarding options and decided to try taking the dogs to the sporting events which I am covering. In particular, a few years ago, Olive enjoyed a trip to the Women's British Open golf, where I strolled into the media centre as if it were some sort of take your dog-child-to-work day. Thankfully most of the members of the press who were there seemed to be dog people, so Olive wandered around, checking copy and generally lifting morale. Although there were also clear lines drawn between certain countries and cultures and, for some, I might as well have come in trailing a donkey or perhaps a couple of pigs. Both of which, I stress, I would also find acceptable.

But, generally, Olive was feted and petted. Indeed such was the love for dogs of Michele, the chief media officer, that she even gave Olive her own accreditation, then got her up on stage to pretend that she was doing a press conference, where she snuffled away at the microphones and was slightly disappointed at the lack of interest in her quotes.

Anyway, more often on trips away I have to make do with other dogs and just count down the days until I am back with our own. With people whom you miss, it is easier – you know that they are aware of where you are and that you will come back. With dogs you worry that they will be wondering where you are and why-oh-why have you abandoned them? Of course, the reality is more likely that they're not doing either of those things – within a few hours they'll just get on with life and their more immediate dog concerns.

But the thing is, I'm not sure that's always the case. Okay, it is for Mabel – she forgets fairly swiftly and at the very most will have a vague flicker of recognition at my name but then, if pressed on the matter, would say, 'I think he's just upstairs at the moment.' Olive, though, is different. When on a trip I'm occasionally sent a photo of her sitting, staring through the hedge and fixing her gaze on the end of our lane. It's a habit of hers when she knows – or hopes – that my car is going to turn in and she can start throwing her head back in noisy celebration at the gate. Or maybe she's just on the lookout for Dee.

Yet I do think that she registers my absence when I'm not there and every now and again something clicks in her head and she thinks, 'Ah yes . . . that guy. Not a bad man overall. Let me just go and see if he's coming back.' It makes me both deeply sad and happy at the same time, and it's something which I thought about a lot when I was out in Japan, and came to know the story of one of the most famous dogs of all.

34. The Tale of the Lonesome Pine

Being a freelance sports broadcaster makes for a decidedly uneven year. It is not nine to five, nor Monday to Friday and it certainly does not abide by a regular calendar.

It is also a fickle business and you are reliant on whichever company you work for holding on to the broadcasting rights for that sport or that event. If one or two disappear then suddenly the weeks on your wallchart can empty. There might be vast deserts to cross before you reach the promised land of a few days' work covering a ten-pin bowling event.

Although I would say that if you are ever approached with the salvation of an offer to host the Stationery Supplier of the Year Awards (Midlands region), you should not answer the email within 0.3 nanoseconds of it arriving. Furthermore, when you have left it as long as you possibly can, try to maintain a calm air and always give the impression that it's going to be difficult to fit them in as you are a pretty big deal and in *significant* demand. As you stare at the giant blank that is your diary, with a moth helpfully turning the page, the charade continues.

'Sure . . . sure . . . Let me just see if I can shuffle things around. Never busier really – which is GREAT of course, but I wouldn't mind a break now and again, hahahahaha . . .' Then, you hold the phone away from your mouth and shout, 'Susan . . . Can we do that important thing for those important people of great importance on Wednesday instead? Difficult I know, but let's try and make it happen.' All this said to Mabel, who is tilting her head and trying to work out what you're talking about. Or even worrying that she's actually meant to call some people.

But then there is the other side of things – the parts of the year into which settle so many of the events that I cover, that it becomes a long stretch going from one to another without a break. Often in the summer when the jigsaw pieces fit neatly together you can find yourself doing forty or fifty days without pause for reflection.

One of the longest spells which I had away from Olive and Mabel came in the autumn of 2019 when I was on the road for two months at various events. It was a tour of golf, athletics and rugby which eventually took me out to Qatar for the World Athletics Championships and then on to Japan for the Rugby World Cup before a week in China covering golf. There is a similar stretch every year – 2020, for example, should have meant two months away from home in July and August, ending with three weeks out in Japan at the Olympic Games. Instead it was months of watching Olive clean her nether regions and wondering if it would be inappropriate to commentate on it.

I was glad to have had my first trip to Japan as it is a fascinating place. Probably not so much to the Japanese, to whom… well, it's just a place – but it is a country that does things in its own, unique way, which to outsiders can seem strange. I had wanted to go there for some time, ever since watching the great Clive James showcase the country, affectionately describing its quirks and curiosities to the western world in his television programmes of the 1980s.

It is also a country of some devotion to dogs although, as with other aspects of life, they view them in their own way. The Japanese clearly love a canine but the trend – as it seems to be with many things – is to the miniature. Dogs in bags, dogs in prams, dogs wearing coats or hats. They seem to be dogs as accessories and are often swept up in the country's affection for the eccentric and cartoonish.

Once when out for a jog in Yoyogi Park, near where we were staying in Tokyo, I saw a dog – not running around, catching a frisbee, chewing a stick or sniffing other dogs. Rather, this proud and noble descendant of the wolf was being pushed around in a buggy while wearing a Superman costume. Everyone there who saw it seemed to consider this perfectly normal behaviour, while the dog itself looked as royally pissed off as you might imagine. Perhaps he had really wanted to be Spider-Man.

But it's one thing which I've always steered away from – dogs in fancy dress. Or any type of dress. This may prompt people to do a deep dive into my social media channels and shame me as they discover that I have shamed my dogs. So yes, full disclosure, I did once put Olive in a running vest from a race I had just done. She may also have worn a scarf at Christmas and indeed you are correct, Mabel was put into a lion wig to mark the Lions v All Blacks rugby encounter a couple of years ago. I even reposted it in the summer of 2020 and then deleted it after I had a little think about myself and the slippery dog-costumed slope I was on. But these have been very rare occurrences.

I've also never been one of those who tends towards the cutesie for dogs. I am not someone who considers dogs his babies or children or in any way think of myself as their 'dad'. I have met other dog walkers who, when I tell Olive or Mabel off for some nefarious act, say in a slightly sing-song voice, 'Ooooohhhh, Daddy is cross with yooooo . . .' To which I am always tempted to reply, 'Sorry, you've misunderstood – we are quite clearly in no way related. Her dad is called Henry and lives in a kennel in Devon.' Don't misunderstand me – I love my dogs dearly, but if I were ever to find myself rushing into a maternity ward to be presented with a Labrador wrapped in a blanket I would consider it something of a disappointment.

Yet in Tokyo a small canine in a pram was a familiar sight – although this may just be a big city thing. And besides, the dog culture of Japan is more than redeemed by a story which I shall tell you now – about the country's most celebrated dog, who was a large, proud and above all faithful beast.

I was staying near Shibuya railway station, which is beside the famous road junction and 'Scramble Crossing'. This is where tens of thousands of people every day make their way across – then stop halfway to take a selfie while making a peace sign and pouting. I often like to think of the number of social media posts around the world at that time which would have been ruined by a scowling Scottish man in the background.

But whenever I reached Shibuya station, bracing myself for the national sport of let's see how many people we can fit on a train, I would always feel the need to pause by the statue which sits at one of the entrances. It represents one of the most famous dogs who has ever lived and one whose name has become a byword for trust and faithfulness in Japan . . . Hachikō.

Hachikō was an Akita – a large breed originating, using the same naming formula as Labradors, from the Akita prefecture in northern Japan and in 1924 he had been brought to Tokyo by a Professor Ueno, who worked at the Imperial University in the city. Each day the professor and Hachikō would head to Shibuya station from where the professor got his train and then Hachikō would hang around all day, possibly at the 1920s Japanese equivalent of Pret A Manger, waiting for his friend and master to return.

One day, very sadly, the professor wasn't able to make the return journey, for the very valid reason that he had expired mid-lecture after suffering a brain haemorrhage. Hachikō waited and waited and when the professor didn't appear, eventually went home wearing a puzzled expression. But what followed was the habit of a lifetime for which Hachikō became known. For almost *ten years*, right up until the dog's own death, he would go to the station every day at the hour of the professor's return train, to sit and wait for his friend and favourite human, who never came back.

Well, if that doesn't tug at your heartstrings . . .

This demonstration of pining canine love might have remained just a local story and curiosity until one of the professor's former students wrote about the loyal dog (and about all Akitas, of which there were only thirty purebred examples remaining at the time). One of his studies was picked up by a national newspaper and the legend of Hachikō grew. People would come to see him at Shibuya station where he sat, continuing his hopeful vigil. The fact that they might occasionally throw him a snack as well probably let him know that he was doing the right thing. Throughout much of his life, and for nearly a century since, he has been used to promote family values in Japan and held up as an example of loyalty and fidelity. He has featured in books, comics, film and television. There is grainy footage of him in later life – where, incidentally, he looks as if he has not refused many edible gifts from passing fans and such is his popularity that when somebody in the 1990s discovered an ancient and scratchy recording of Hachikō barking, millions tuned in to hear it on the radio. Imagine the likes and retweets if social media had been around, with perhaps even a thumbs-up emoji from the Emperor himself.

Many countries appear to have a similar story of dog faithfulness. There was the aptly named Fido in Italy, whose owner was killed in an air-raid during the Second World War, but for fourteen years went to meet the same bus which his owner had always caught, to wait for his return. Then there is Greyfriars Bobby, the Skye terrier who has his own statue in Edinburgh after a dozen years of supposedly sitting on his departed master's grave. Or the Indian dog Waghya, who rather took it to extremes by leaping into the funeral pyre of his human, Shivaji, a seventeenth-century warrior-king.

I suspect that some of these stories have been stretched in the telling as parables. Not all though – Hachikō and Fido are certainly true – and what is clear is that dogs can have emotional bonds to us as strong as ours are to them. It's just that some have set a higher standard for all other dogs to follow, because I have to concede that at the moment we are unlikely to have future generations telling stories to their children, who listen in wide-eyed wonder to something along the lines of:

'Gather round children . . . This statue is dedicated to the amazing story of a very loyal dog, Olive, who briefly looked through some foliage when her owner was away at a golf tournament, before heading back in for dinner and a snooze.'

35. The Wise Man of Fuji

I couldn't possibly leave Japan without telling you of one of my most memorable days on a mountain. Some of you may even have read this book in the expectation that there would be plenty of the steep stuff. So, in reward for your Hachikō-esque loyalty, let me move from the most celebrated dog in Japan to the most famous mountain. Indeed, one of the most famous in the world.

In the same way that I gravitate towards dogs on foreign trips, I will also always try and find a peak to scale. For example, at the Olympics in Rio de Janeiro there was Pedra da Gávea – a damp and muddy climb through tropical jungle until you emerge, greasy and perspiring on the finest peak of all those which encircle that chaotic city and seem to herd it towards the sea. You even look down on the outstretched arms of Christ the Redeemer as He stands above the faithful – on the beaches and in the bars and above the hundreds of thousands of ramshackle houses which lie beyond the cameras of the tourists, creeping up the steep slopes as if trying to escape.

Even for the faithless there is a sort of spirituality to be found in the mountains and after the US Open at Torrey Pines in California in 2008 (where Tiger Woods hobbled to victory on a broken leg), there was a trip to Yosemite. It is a place where you crane your neck, constantly gazing up at nature's Sistine Chapel and it was there that I spent an unforgettable day on Half Dome. Out of season, before any tourists and without the assistance cables in place, trusting the dry sticky granite as I crept up the steep and smooth curve to share the summit only with an equally daring man from Cleveland and a foraging marmot, briefly distracted from his work. Similarly, Alpine expeditions might follow if I got out to the golf at Crans-sur-Sierre and if on holiday in Australia we would occasionally head to the Grampians in Victoria to scale the very honestly named Mount Abrupt.

There is often a wonderful frankness to the geographical naming procedure in Australia. It's no different, I suppose, to the simple Red Peaks or Big Hills in Scotland, only they sound more exotic in Gaelic. Apart from Mount Abrupt, other Australian prominences include Round Mountain in New South Wales, Clear Hill in Tasmania and the exquisitely named Mount Superbus in Queensland, which depending on which syllable you choose to stress is either the Latin word for proud, or awesome public transport.

But my favourite would undoubtedly be Mount Disappointment,

which lies about forty miles north of Melbourne. In 1824 explorers Hamilton Hume and William Hovell were hoping that from its summit they might be able to see Port Phillip Bay, where Melbourne now sits. Unfortunately the view was obscured by an abundance of trees and, in addition to that, Hume suffered an unpleasant injury to his groin. So, they settled on the name Mount Disappointment which, bearing in mind all that had happened, could have been much worse.

Some countries don't offer anything too exciting in the way of hilly diversions, not even a Mount Average, or you simply might not have the time, but if you are in Japan and you do have a spare day, there is one mountain which draws you in. And so it was that I found myself on Fuji.

Lying, as it does, on the very lively Pacific Ring of Fire, Japan, in fact, has plenty of mighty peaks and I had initially planned to take myself off to the Minami Alps in the week before the quarter-finals. Scotland had generously lost to the host nation for the greater good of the tournament and – impressively organised though it may be – I fancied a retreat from the overwhelming crush of Tokyo. Yet, like many of the plans I make, it was overly ambitious – plotted on a map that bore no relation to the reality of the landscape or the journey required to get there. So instead I altered my objective and headed for Fuji.

It is an iconic image of Japan that graces almost every postcard with its perfect conical structure, usually seen from a speeding bullet train and often with a sharply defined snowline which sits like icing on the top of this long-dormant volcano. It's a big mountain as well – rising for almost 12,500 feet in splendid isolation about sixty miles south-west of Tokyo and it is seen as a rite of passage for thousands of people who flock every year to its ash-covered slopes.

That was one of the reasons why I had been reluctant to do it. Climbing in any sort of mass company is really not my thing. One person, perhaps two people if I'm feeling particularly outgoing, is acceptable. Two dogs more than acceptable. But the idea of trooping up in the kind of crowds that you see on some popular mountains in high season defeats my whole purpose of climbing.

The question of why we head for the hills will bring a different response depending on who you ask. For some, it is a target to reach – perhaps knocking off as many Munros or 4,000-metre peaks of the Alps as possible, or even a Himalayan giant. While for others it is the challenge of scaling the hardest rock faces or testing yourself against brutal conditions. My motivation is sometimes a little bit of all of those things, but above all it is in finding some quiet.

The most famous answer given to that sort of question came from the great, and ultimately tragic, George Mallory – pioneer of early attempts to climb Mount Everest who, after one of his first expeditions ended in retreat, was asked by a newspaper reporter why he had wanted to climb the world's highest peak.

'Because it's there,' he is reported to have replied.

For me, 'Because it's there' can be extended to 'Because it's there, and the rest of the world is not'. I would no more climb to the top of Ben Nevis or Snowdon by the tourist route on a busy Saturday than listen to Mabel give a three-hour presentation on earthenware pottery (although that would have a certain novelty value for the first few minutes). I also understand that a huge number of people really enjoy communal hillwalking and, hey, if those folk are getting exercise in the great outdoors then that can only be good. I'm just looking for something a bit more roomy. And, in that vein, pictures of Fuji during the summer months filled me with horror, with queues of people barely able to move.

Fortunately a way to avoid such a throng is possible. There is a Japanese saying which translates as, 'A wise man climbs Fuji once. Only a fool would climb it twice.' There is also an old Scottish saying which goes, 'A wise man climbs Fuji when it is technically closed so that he has the entire mountain to himself.'

Rules being rules, Fuji is out of bounds from the end of September until the start of July, something which I found extraordinary but again, Japan is an extraordinary place. There is a devotion to order and safety which means that snow is considered to be something of a slip hazard and therefore the whole of the mountain is shut down, just as it gets more interesting.

I would stress here that it is not illegal or forbidden to climb out of season. It is simply a sort of recommendation which, in this rule-obeying country, is usually more than enough. Indeed, when I told our translator of my plans to climb Fuji, she gave a look of concern which leaped across language barriers. Then, after a bus ride down from Tokyo, I checked into the tiny hotel in the town of Gotemba at the foot of the mountain and the smiling receptionist presented me with my room key, held in both hands like a rare treasure, and asked if I was there on business.

'Yes indeed. The business of climbing Fuji,' I said cheerily, adding a scuttling motion with my fingers and pointing out of the window in the wrong direction. She understood anyway, because suddenly the smile disappeared and a rather grave atmosphere descended as she gathered in her colleagues to discuss how best to deal with me.

A more senior and rather sombre figure then came over. 'Fuji is . . . uhh . . . not possible,' he said, as if delivering the news that a close relative had departed and I started to wonder if I really had wasted my time coming down here and, indeed, wasted energy and suitcase space carrying winter climbing gear through the heat of Doha a couple of weeks before. For those reasons alone I was determined to carry on. Besides, how can you close a mountain?

Well, thankfully, in Japan the method seems to be by placing a small plastic cone across the starting points of the four trails that head up from different sides of the volcano. My solution to this closure the next day – with a quiet and respectful apology to my hosts – was to move the small cone slightly to the side and start climbing.

I had been dropped off at eight-thirty in the morning by a very cheery taxi driver and had somehow, through a combination of Google Translate and pointing at my watch, explained that I would like to be picked up at five-thirty that evening, in the same place. By that time it would already be dark, but I was leaving myself plenty of room for the climb. I had also naturally chosen the best weather day available to me that week with sunshine promised on the peak of the mountain. Although for the next few hours I would come to view that weather forecast with more than a fair amount of suspicion.

In October, until the cold, clearer winter air makes an appearance, Japan on the Pacific side can be a rather damp place. I was effectively climbing in a cloud, able to see no more than about thirty yards ahead as I plodded up the slopes of ash, which gave way slightly with every step. And, while it wasn't raining, my jacket was becoming soaked simply with the amount of moisture in the air. Combine that with a fairly perky wind and the going was chilly.

This was the kind of climbing where you just have to find a rhythm and grind it out – one foot in front of the other, over and over and over again. Then repeat. And once in a while, stop to turn around and marvel at no view whatsoever. The only way of measuring progress made was the altimeter on my watch and the basic shelters, or stations as they are called, placed at intervals on the higher reaches of the trail.

In the summer the stations are crucial for many of those who make their slow way up Fuji – somewhere to rest and replenish if you might not be the fittest mountain goat. Today they were a sorry sight. Typhoon Hagibis had just torn through the country and they had taken a beating. Even in a place where hundred-mile-an-hour winds are not that rare, the wooden buildings and corrugated roofs had suffered. Just past one of the final stations is where I encountered the only other life I saw on Fuji that day. The rumble of an engine grew louder and out of the mist emerged the caterpillar tracks of the kind of vehicle that smooths down the snow on ski slopes. Here it was flattening down the ash – I imagined for access rather than aesthetics.

The driver looked at me with the same curious gaze that Clive James had received from surrounding businessmen while trying karaoke in a Tokyo bar all those years before. From the warmth of his cabin he was now waving frantically, clearly suggesting that I shouldn't be there. I decided to employ the tactic of pretending that I had misunderstood, gave him a thumbs-up in reply and a cry of 'LOVELY DAY', then an exaggerated cheery wave before I ploughed on.

Except, none of it at this point was lovely. It was getting colder and seemed if anything to be getting darker. It was certainly getting harder with every few hundred feet gained. Going from sea level to anything over 12,000 feet in a single day will take its toll on your lungs.

But then the wondrous happened. If you know that moment where you break through the clouds in a plane shortly after taking off, then that is what this was like. In slower motion of course, but the first rays of sun broke weakly through the shroud which covered me, then grew stronger and within a few minutes I was standing above a slightly crumpled white carpet and looking up at the huge rim of the volcanic crater, sharp-edged against a perfect blue sky. I had climbed out of a world dank and grey, into one bright and vivid.

It's at these times that, loner or not, I do wish that I had someone there with me, to share that experience. I would say I wished I had Olive and Mabel there as well, but I'm not sure they could appreciate the ethereal beauty of it. Besides, this harsh volcanic rock harboured no life to chew at and would not be at all kind on their paws, even if it would exfoliate them superbly.

Rejuvenated and now floating with such a feeling of immense height, the final few hundred feet were a joy, picking my way over the ice-covered rocks and through a small wooden shrine which marks the top of the path, on to the edge of the crater itself. And, standing beside that vast mouth – about half a mile across and over six hundred feet deep – all I can say is that when this part of Fuji was formed around ten thousand years ago, it must have been quite a firework display.

There is actually a fair amount up there. A rudimentary café or two, shuttered and locked for the long off-season, then further round, at the point which marks the actual summit, an old disused weather station.

I also found a number of shrines dedicated to Sakuya-hime – or Sengen – who, in Japanese mythology, is the blossom princess and, apparently, the reason why we don't live long enough. The story goes that the god Ninigi chose her to marry rather than her sister, the rock princess Iwa-Naga. Their father, Oho-Yama, reluctantly agreed – no doubt accepting that, as a deity, Ninigi had decent prospects – but thereafter human lives would be delicate and fleeting like the sakura, or cherry blossom, rather than strong and enduring like stones.

Sakuya-hime is also the goddess of Fuji and all volcanoes; the belief is that she will prevent Fuji from erupting again. Similar shrines in her honour were a familiar sight in the Kirishima mountains of Japan's southern tip, but had recently been destroyed by volcanic eruptions – a theological quandary which I chose not to dwell on as I gazed into the mouth of the sleeping giant.

Indeed, the whole place was dormant and it was all mine. Of another soul there was not a glimpse – nobody else there to experience one of the greatest sights I have ever seen. With the enormous crater at my back I looked out on the clouds, rolling in waves to the coast itself, where they broke upon the shore and just beyond them the glint of sunlight on the waters of the Pacific. Quite often in the mountains you don't have to believe in anything to still feel something.

Suddenly I realised that I had rather lost track of time. Fingertips were beginning to give up the fight after being out of gloves for so much photo-taking. I had even tried to justify my ascent in what was essentially a few days of prep for the weekend rugby matches by filming myself doing a short preview of the quarter-finals. I then searched for a signal on my phone as I contemplated trying to FaceTime Olive and Mabel to tell them where I was. But I accepted that it would have been lost on them and, after six hours of climbing and an hour of gazing around in awe which I sorely wished could have lasted far longer, it was time to go.

In fact, it was well past that time as the descent became a race against the light. The massive pyramid shadow of Fuji was stretching further in front of me onto the white layer of clouds and I realised that the sun may be down before I was. The cloud level had also dropped, revealing the huge flank of the mountain which hadn't been visible on the ascent and letting me know just how far I still had to go.

But this would be nothing like the struggle of the way up. Such is the uniform consistency of the soft ash on this part of the mountain that you can practically bounce down, as if on a sand dune. In fact, I had learned that the record for a descent of this side was a full nine thousand feet in about forty minutes.

Digging heels deep into the cinders I was making a speedy descent myself, but it soon became clear that I was also going to create on each heel pad a blister so enormous that it might feature in any number of medical journals. Still, it had to be done if I were to meet my taxi driver and uphold any sort of British reputation for punctuality in the country where it is an art form. But it was looking unlikely because in this race, just a mile or so from the finish, the night had won.

Fuji is rather unsettling when one is totally alone in the dark. I was only glad that I was not descending by the trail through the forest on the northern slopes of the mountain which the Japanese have long believed to be the home of spirits and demons and sadly, in more recent times, has become the favoured final destination for those who wish to join the spirits. I was ninety degrees further round the mountain and my descent was treeless, but still as it grew black and I entered the cloud it was an unearthly place. 'Ah, of course,' I said to myself. 'Lack of daylight . . . probably another reason why they close it.'

It shouldn't have been a problem and I actually quite like climbing in the dark, but now, back in the low clouds my head torch was pointless, merely lighting up the millions of drops of moisture like bright lights on a car in the fog and only making visibility worse. So it had to be switched off and the blackness was near total.

At this point I needed my dogs and their rather sharper night-vision – or, at the very least, their facial whiskers – to feel my way down. As it was, my week-old stubble proved decidedly ineffective and I wandered from side to side and into a number of scrubby bushes. Now my only certainty was that I was descending – although sometimes I wasn't even quite sure of that. But just when my wailing was enough to scare off any nearby demons and I was considering setting up home here, a light appeared, no more than a few hundred yards away. Two lights, in fact – headlights, with a tiny green 'Taxi' sign shining above. And so I was guided back to the car park.

The driver was smiling as broadly as when I left him and was also perhaps impressed with my time-keeping.

'Good-good?' he asked, with a thumbs-up.

'Good. Very good,' I replied as I gratefully threw my gear in the back and climbed in.

And it really had been good. Better than good. A memory which remains as vivid now as it was then and in the following days. Images and emotions so deeply imprinted that even with the fading of time they'll remain.

The more earthly concern of the Rugby World Cup continued. I had to leave two weeks later to head to a golf tournament in Shanghai, but I had got all that I wanted and more from this trip, which by the end had felt just a bit too long away. But, again, there are no complaints. I knew I would be back at home for the next few weeks and, besides, it is part of the job – a job which allows me to travel to faraway places, to see incredible sights and occasionally to climb very special mountains.

When I finally did return from that trip, to see Olive and Mabel for the first time in almost two months, the welcome I got was quite something. I had looked forward to it as every country passed slowly below me on the long flight back. I thought about it as I stood in immigration and at the baggage reclaim. I was practically bouncing as I drove home from the airport and the moment when I finally burst in through the door it lived up to all expectations as my own two Hachikōs sprang to life.

There was that fraction of a second of contemplation and then an explosion of joy. Five solid minutes of wuffing and whining and yelping and wagging followed – some of it even from the dogs – before we all eventually settled down. I collapsed on the sofa and Olive came and sat next to me, content that I was here and now staying close enough so that I shouldn't escape from her again. Then she turned to look at me with eyes that said:

'Very good to have you back. What news from the supermarket?'

36. Where You Go, We Will Follow

Sometimes you have to take every opportunity which presents itself to get to the mountains. You do so if that small weather window opens up. Or if you have the time off. Or perhaps you get the feeling that *everything* is about to shut down, so get out there now. And in that rare instance you really go for it.

In early March 2020 there was more than a certain uneasiness about the way things were developing. Yet in the mountains, conditions had developed quite beautifully. February in Scotland had seen a huge amount of snowfall in the west, with a regular conveyor belt of Atlantic fronts sweeping in and crashing into cold air – as if winter were apologising profusely and providing restitution for the miserable mild and wet months of December and January. Combine those factors with a few days off and a decent forecast and it was an easy decision to make. Head north.

I would be meeting up with Iain Cameron again to try a bit of ski-touring, but I had an extra day so decided to take Olive and Mabel on a wander. Which is the gentle, understated way of describing our bonus walk.

We happy three headed into the Munros of the Monadhliath (the 'Grey Mountains') just outside Newtonmore. As with the hills surrounding the Drumochter Pass these are very easy to reach, sitting not too far from the edges of the town – yet, just a short distance beyond the last of the houses and we were into another world. What's more, an almost entirely unpopulated world.

I am forever thankful that an irregular job does mean that I can disappear into the mountains at irregular times and miss the weekend crowds. There are also a huge number of fair-weather hillwalkers who take the Japanese approach and consider the mountains firmly off-limits when winter comes around. I do feel that they're missing out, but I wasn't unhappy at their decision-making as we left an empty parking area and headed off down a farm track and into the silence.

I say silence, but sadly I had fallen victim that day to an ear-worm – one of those songs which you might hear only briefly but then can't remove from your head. You are more prone to the symptoms if you are involved in extended and solitary exercise – perhaps a jog, or a cycle, or a swim, or indeed an eighteen-mile walk through the hills. So it was that as we headed into the painting – a scene of a wild, almost arctic beauty – the crunch of the snow and the rhythm of my increasingly hard breathing was accompanied by Ralph McTell, who was quite insistent on telling me about the Streets of London and the various troubles to be found there.

As far as I'm aware dogs don't suffer from anything similar – probably because more than one thought in their head would cause overload. Trying to hum a tune, for example, would mean them forgetting how to walk. And their heads are usually fully occupied with other distractions, although thankfully on this occasion their options were limited, as whatever sheep, hares, deer or any other creature had donated to the landscape was well covered in snow.

I must say that Mabel is more often the culprit in this respect, seeing every pile of droppings as akin to a free bowl of peanuts left on a bar, although probably slightly more hygienic. This is where basic recall training should make my life considerably easier as I would summon them back to my side with a commanding and authoritative whistle or cry. Instead I wave a bag of cheese or sausages at the dogs and let them make their own decision on the matter. And I have to say that if I were the manufacturers of Mini-Babybels I wouldn't be overjoyed to hear that it's only a marginal decision.

Thankfully, on this day, no snack-waving was necessary as, from about a thousand feet in height, all earthly temptations were buried. So we continued, largely uninterrupted except for Ralph still absolutely sure that he was going to change my mind about something. Every now and again we would stop for refreshment and I would sit for a few minutes simply revelling in our situation. The sky was clear, the sun was bright and just strong enough, as we had crept into the very edge of spring, to keep us warm.

Sometimes we would stop by a burn – or on top of a burn, which I would locate by a combination of my peerless map-reading skills and also by one leg crashing through the covering and a boot plunging into the icy water beneath. Mabel would look shocked and, after I assured that her that it was entirely planned, I would try to encourage the dogs to rehydrate, tossing snowballs into the clear water in the hope that Olive might hop in and have a drink. But the sole occupant of her head then was the object thrown and you could see the cogs and gears slowly turning as she tried to work out how that ball had magically disappeared.

And so it went on, hard and heavy progress breaking trail and disturbing more mountain hares than I have seen in a single day – perfectly camouflaged until we approached and they revealed themselves to dogs who were first confused and then deeply interested. Lepus timidus fully lived up to their name and so too Olive and Mabel of the genus Huntus pointlus. There is nothing that more accurately demonstrates the optimism of dogs than the sight of a hare, travelling at Mach 3 and being pursued (if that's even a fair description) by two dogs progressing only with laboured arcs through the snow and wondering why they seem to have lost a yard or two of pace. Yet still they would return with a wag and a face that says, 'Now THAT, my friend, was close . . .'

Once more, though, I was a bit concerned about energy expended as this was shaping up to become another long and arduous day. The deep snow meant that we had already given a lot of effort and there would be no point in heading straight back after one Munro. It wouldn't shorten the distance greatly and we may as well hope for firmer snow up on the high ground, grit our teeth and complete the loop.

The first of our achievements, Càrn Dearg was dramatic, a summit which sits like the prow of a ship above Glen Ballach, where we had walked in, and here the wind was brisk. All the way up the flank I had worked hard, kicking my boots into the snow to make steps – the staircase leading up for six hundred feet. Now, as I stopped for a moment, just a hundred yards or so from the cairn which marked the top, the sweat soaking my top started to freeze and I quickly dropped the rucksack and dug out my jacket, hanging on as it whipped in the wind like a red sail on the rigging. I knew the dogs could last longer than me, so their coats only came out once I was safely into my own extra layer. Then it was time to take a few photos, with four ears now flapping like my coat, turn ninety degrees and start the trek of five miles across the plateau of the Monadhliath.

On this sort of terrain there is nothing really to do but admire the views if you can and settle in for the long haul – with steps as short and light as possible in a futile attempt to remain on the surface. There is very seldom soft snow up high in Scotland – it is always wind-scoured which leaves a firm crust that is nevertheless incapable of supporting a substantial weight. Fortunately for Olive and Mabel, the tipping point seems to be somewhere just above medium-to-large dog size as they are generally fine to tiptoe along whereas I would always have a brief, happy moment of believing it might hold me, before I was in up to my knees. Step, hope, sink . . . step, hope, sink, like some sort of pessimistic life metaphor. Over and over again with no end in sight.

Olive and Mabel had at least fallen into a more disciplined formation – one behind me and one in front, with Mabel occasionally looking up with furrowed brow and a questioning stare, hoping for some explanation for all of this. But I was coping with the long, heavy trudge by disappearing into a reverie, forcibly ejecting 'Streets of London' from my head and instead thinking of the list and the achievements of the greatest dog mountaineers of all time.

As it happens, hillwalking and climbing records don't seem to be maintained in quite as much detail for our four-legged companions as for us, but the dog walker to beat all others is probably a man called Hamish Brown – someone whom dogs talk about amongst themselves in awed tones. 'You belong to Hamish Brown? Well . . . good luck. Make sure you stretch properly . . .'

Hamish is a legendary figure of the Scottish hillwalking scene. He was the first person to summit every Munro in a single connected trip – 112 days for all of them in 1974, but he was seldom alone. He was accompanied by Kitchy – his Shetland sheepdog and one of the very few in the country who didn't belong to my grandmother. It was Kitchy who became the first dog to 'compleat' all of the Munros, with another one belonging to Hamish, Storm, also marking that achievement later. One thing is for sure, his pets did not lack for exercise and I wouldn't be at all surprised if he also put his guinea pigs through some fairly strenuous yoga.

I don't know how many of the mountains climbed by Kitchy or Storm were done in the snow, but there wouldn't be many breeds better designed for the purpose than Shetland sheepdogs – light-weight but hardy and with the thickest of coats. If you were to ask me which breeds might be the least successful in that environment, then bullmastiffs for their sheer unwillingness to participate or perhaps dachshunds, who would lack nothing in effort, but would disappear beneath the white, with the only glimpse a helpful peri-scope rising above the surface.

A good few other dogs have achieved the feat of Munro-completion. Kerry, a boxer dog, did it in 2009, and perhaps the most heart-warming achievement was that of a spaniel called Genghis who, after his owner had died, was given to a chap called Mac Wright. Genghis himself was already ten years old and probably planning a gentle retirement with occasional rounds of golf or a bit of gardening. But instead his new owner started climbing Munros with him and within three years they had managed the lot. Like all dogs there was a little bit of help on the Inaccessible Pinnacle – a thin blade of rock at the heart of the Cuillin on Skye. A photo shows Genghis being hauled up in a bag with an enormous loss of dignity but, I'm sure, a certain sense of achievement too.

All these stories confirm that a dog will do what you ask of them. It is extremely unlikely that a single cat has ever climbed a Munro, as they would be prone to say, 'Now what, in the name of God, would I want to do that for?' Yet most dogs (I think I'll exclude bullmastiffs) will simply follow their owners wherever they are asked. This is why some people might wonder if it is too much for the dogs and should they be put through it? Well, as long you are sensible and observant, I can't think of any better life for a dog to have or any better way to build a bond and make memories that will last for a lifetime.

So, let me tell you finally, during my own hauling of a partly willing Olive and Mabel across a windswept and wild plateau, about the finest mountaineering achievement by a dog, which demonstrates exactly why they may be the greatest creatures on earth.

At the end of 2018, a group of climbers were making an attempt on Baruntse, not far from Everest – one of the lesser peaks of that part of the Himalaya. 'Lesser' being entirely relative here, as Baruntse still soars to over 23,000 feet. While crossing a glacier at 18,000 feet they discovered that their party had increased by the factor of dog. A stray, not uncommon among the villages of Nepal and the lower slopes of the Khumbu Valley, had decided that it might be in her interest to join the expedition and simply kept on climbing alongside her new human friends. The Sherpas tried to shoo her back down but the more dog-oriented folk among the group, led by an American called Don Wargowsky, rather enjoyed her company and were thinking more of her welfare as she continued with the ascent. She doggedly (as you might expect) tackled any difficulties presented, of which there were plenty. The humans were depending on fixed ropes to get past these tricky sections while Mera (freshly named after another peak which they had just climbed) relied on claws, sure-footedness and sheer determination. (Wargowsky wrote a great blog all about Mera – which is where I read of her epic adventure.)

This part of the story had reminded me of a time when I was doing a winter climb on An Stùc, part of the Lawers range on the north side of Loch Tay and I realised that I had left my crampons in the car. The final three hundred feet of that mountain is a reason-ably pointy cone and I only struggled up with the help of a couple of ice axes, but slipping constantly in my bare boots. Alongside me, Olive and Mabel scuttled up and down, their paws and claws working beautifully, mocking my efforts.

Mera was in a far more precarious environment, but still coped with everything thrown at her – and there was a lot. She had to spend a couple of nights on her own at 20,000 feet, digging out a hollow in the snow and curling up after she had been reluctant to come back down the difficult sections (down-climbing is always more intimidating for man or beast). She was then tied up in a lower camp for her own safety but refused to stay when told – which sounds familiar – and re-joined the group for the final summit push. On the way she escaped a slide down a gully when caught by Wargowsky, who realised that she was getting herself in trouble by trying to keep close to him. So he then diverted to a ridge which would be more awkward for him, but more manageable for her.

They also sat it out for a few days of fifty-mile-an-hour winds before Wargowsky and the others headed for the summit, thankful to be leaving Mera sleeping soundly in the tent. Seven hours of climbing later and after managing their way along knife-edge ridges and up challenging sixty-degree walls of ice, the humans looked back to see this remarkable dog climbing up to meet them again. And so together they went on to the summit. It was, at 23,389 feet, almost certainly the greatest height ever climbed by a dog.

The key thing from Wargowsky's telling of the adventure is not just the beauty of the dog doing everything to stay with this human to whom she had grown so attached, but that he was likewise prepared to do everything to help her in return. Bashing out steps in the snow to make life easier for his new companion, splitting his limited food with her and rigging a harness to help her abseil the seemingly impossible sections on the way back down, before steering her through any further difficulties on the long walk out to civilisation. In the end Mera had firmly won over the Sherpas who now considered her lucky and one of them, the base camp manager, adopted her and gave her a new name – Baru – after the mountain which she had scaled. She now lives happily with him in Kathmandu, despite the obvious unpleasantness of that name to all canines.

And that's the point. Dogs don't ask for much – given just a little bit of love and food, they will follow you to the ends, or the top, of the earth. I'm sure that a dog will never climb Everest, but my goodness if they were asked they would give it their best shot. A cat, at the very most, would agree to wait in Base Camp, promising to keep an eye on things there. And when the rest of the expedition returned bedraggled and half-dead from their summit attempt, they would find no camp remaining, only a note in a cat-scrawl under a rock that said: 'Got bored. Gone back to village. Sold tents.'

Anyway, I use all these stories to try and explain the connection that I feel – as I'm sure all these human climbers do with their dogs as they traipse through the mountains – and the total trust that the dogs put in their companions.

As we kept on going in the Monadhliath, step after step, I was rudely awakened from my reverie on stoic and overachieving dogs by Mabel complaining about something – perhaps the two-degree increase in gradient as we made it to the next Munro, Carn Sgulain, which is really no more than a slight rise in the plateau. Then we doubled back before heading on to number three – A' Chailleach – which I had looked forward to as a vantage point of some repute. Sadly for all of us, it will remain only in repute as the cloud which had been boiling up in the glens and chasing us across the plateau eventually caught and swallowed one man and two dogs.

It was high time to get back in any case, as it had been constant hard work for eight hours with no let up. I thought of the skis which I would use tomorrow, sitting redundant in my car and gazed longingly at the perfect run which would have given two thousand feet of descent in five minutes – but only if I turned my heart to stone and chose to ignore the flapping ears behind me, trying desperately to keep up and whimpering as I slid out of sight. The extra weight for the walk in had turned me against the idea of skis. Now I was their most devoted fan and imagined how easy life would have been, as I instead plunged down through the snow for an hour or so, which eventually became a bit softer and then broke into patches as the heather and boggier ground started to take over. After another half-hour of trudging, with boots being sucked into the peaty mud and Mabel, having sunk in up to her chest, now looking like a walking pint of stout, we eventually found ourselves back at the car. I then insisted that

Mabel should paddle into the nearby burn to smarten herself up a bit for the journey.

It was then just a short hop to the bed & breakfast outside the village of Kingussie and once there I prepared the dogs' dinner (preparation being getting their bowls and pouring food in), but while doing so I was suddenly startled by the sight of Mabel, as something very strange had happened to her eyes.

For a moment I rather panicked and wondered if it might be some sort of snow-blindness, caused by a whole day of the sun's reflection bouncing off the brilliant white surface. But I had been assured that with the different way canine eyes work, they just don't suffer from the condition in the way that humans do. I then realised that there was nothing *wrong* with her eyes – it's just that they weren't in precisely the place you might expect them to be. Or at least the pupils weren't – they had rolled back in her head. She was falling asleep while sitting up, nodding off even as she sat there holding her knife and fork.

So I accepted that this time I might have worn her out and decided to see how things were the next morning before making a decision on another climb. I told her all of this as I gently shook her awake and steered her in the direction of her bowl.

Then we slept – properly and impressively, fatigue meaning I managed it even in spite of the relentless sound of two dogs snoring. And also Ralph McTell, still there in my head, tuning up for one more rendition.

37. The Last Waltz

All I can say is that the recovery powers of a young Labrador are something to behold. Give them ten hours of sleep and they will be ready to sniff the world once more. Consequently, the next morning Mabel was bouncing around and looked perfectly willing to move to Nepal and open a climbing shop.

It was my own energy reserves which were flagging but they were soon restored by breakfast. The dogs had already eaten, after which Olive had left some negative comments in the visitor's book, since she had been subject to some deeply offensive language from one of the collies which belonged to the owners. In the meantime collie number two was holding down Mabel, who had rolled on to her back to make it clear that she was a lover not a fighter. Neither of the dogs of this establishment seemed to have quite grasped the finer points of the hospitality industry.

Although it must be said that the resident dogs were very amiable towards me as I ate breakfast and were clearly hoping that their politeness might be rewarded, at first staring and then, when their owner went back into the kitchen, deciding that they could risk taking our relationship to the next level by gently nudging my thigh with a persistent nose. At any other time I might have been won over by their perfomance, but the memory of them swearing at Olive and turning Mabel upside down was still fresh. So instead I ignored them and perhaps even exaggerated my approving noises for their benefit as I tackled approximately fourteen courses of outstanding quality and many thousands of calories.

And so it was a heavier but revitalised party which got into the car to reach the starting point for today's outing. We would make our way along the very scenic road which takes you from the centre of the Highlands past Loch Laggan and eventually reaches Fort William in the west, but stopped about halfway to climb a sizeable mountain of a very steady and uniform gradient called Chno Dearg. Heading up and down from the north side, it would be ideal for snow depth and for trying ski-touring, which was the main goal of the day.

Iain was waiting in the small parking area, a couple of miles down a single-track road and Olive was delighted to renew his acquaintance. Mabel's memory for such things doesn't seem quite as impressive and, despite having already climbed with him a few times, she politely asked who he was and what he did. Then I took about forty minutes to perform the simple task of strapping skis and boots to the side of my rucksack and we set off.

The name Chno Dearg means 'red nut' although today it was almost entirely white, but still with enough of a walk-in to lift the heart rate early on, which was already operating at a higher level due to having ingested several puddings before nine a.m. I was straining under the rucksack and the added ski-weight and at the same time holding the leads of two dogs who both rather fancied heading in different directions to say hello to the sheep around us. I consoled myself that this was not going to be as epic and energy-sapping as the day before and that it was not far to reach the snow, when I would be able to have skis on my feet.

Soon past the sheep and unshackled, Olive and Mabel careered around, although perhaps slightly less frantically than usual and Iain and I chatted about various things, but conversation ultimately kept returning to this strange virus which, it appeared, would shortly have a great effect on us all. The theme of the day was very much, enjoy this while we can.

And so we did. Reaching the point where the first few patches of snow tenuously connected through the clumps of heather, we stepped into the skis which already had skins attached and left bags containing our walking boots lying on the ground – taking a mental photo of the terrain so we would find them again and confident that out here in the hills, even if one or two people came along, they would remain undisturbed.

Mabel, however, was becoming very much disturbed as we started to make progress up the hill. This is not uncommon as she expresses misgivings about anything which deviates from her idea of normal or conventional. To be clear, this is a considerable list to which we could now add humans sliding along on giant feet. She seemed to be particularly troubled by the *sound* of the skis – the high-pitched, drawn-out swish of the skins sliding on the snow 'cheeeoooo . . . cheeeoooo . . . cheeeoooo . . .' was almost like the mewl of a cat or a bird of prey. Whether she thought that both were nearby, or perhaps that they were in league with the lion chasing us I'm not sure, but she was certainly becoming deeply vexed about something.

In fact I do remember once, on a climb with the dogs, seeing a golden eagle circling above – one of the most majestic sights of the mountains as it wheeled around, riding on invisible thermals. I knew that the prey of these enormous birds weighed at most about five kilos – but I had visions of an ambitious one setting sights on Mabel as it might a particularly fat hare.

There was not a bird in sight here on Chno Dearg, but Mabel was still offering a constant whine and skipping about nervously. I decided now was not the time to attach the GoPro and switch it on, for fear that she might explode.

As ever in such a situation, just to confirm that it wasn't too cold, or the spindrift perhaps stinging too much as it blew around at dog height, I looked to Olive to see if I could detect any sign of distress there, but she was trotting happily along, fully enjoying her day out. And so I reached the obvious conclusion that Mabel was an idiot.

The best thing to do in these whimpering situations is not to comfort her, tempting though it might be. Telling her in soothing tones that everything is alright would only reinforce her thought that something had previously *not* been alright and she was correct to worry. Instead, with a stuff-and-nonsense air and a matter-of-fact tone, you tell her to toughen up a bit, think of Baru in the Himalaya and get on with it.

Which, thankfully, she did. And it was marvellous. It was turning out to be not quite the sun-blessed snow climb of the day before, but it still had a certain drama to it. For much of the ascent the snow was blowing around on the surface like shifting sand across the dunes of a desert and Iain, with a grand eye for a photo, got down low to capture a shot where I'm flanked by Olive and Mabel. It will always be one of my favourites of the three of us in the mountains.

Then there was the moment where we reached the summit, turned round, changed the setting on the ski-binding and saw the dogs practically rubbing their eyes in disbelief as we disappeared down the slope at high speed.

I have to give Mabel her due – she at least made an effort to keep up, stumbling down through the snow whereas Olive, with the wisdom of her years, decided to trot steadily behind, relying on the belief that one, or both of us, might occasionally fall. I confess that Iain and I repaid her faith a couple of times, although I would also point out that my crash was due to the fact that I was twisted round filming Mabel as I descended – and if you would like a glimpse of Mabel's game effort to keep up on that descent, then by all means head to YouTube and have a search for 'Mabel's Dream'.

We paused at the bealach (a col or saddle between peaks) for a quick look up at the flank of the neighbouring Munro, Stob Coire Sgrìodain, which overlooks Loch Treig. It had been part of the day's plan and the summit was flitting in and out of the clouds, but it might well have fine views over to Ben Nevis. What's more it looked like there was a fun climb up an easy gully, but then we considered the two smallest members of the party, who were panting away beside us, having just caught up. And with two big days in the mountains, both Olive and Mabel had done more than enough. So we headed down.

All too quickly it was over and we were back at the snowline, finding our stash of boots and heading down to the cars, with more than one or two glances over our shoulders at the unclimbed mountain which by now, I noticed with some regret, was taunting us with a clear summit. I am constantly told 'the mountains will always be there' and I know they will – it's just I'm never sure when, or if, *I* am going to be back and I know that some mountains will remain forever unclimbed. But it had still been another rich experience and as I sorted out my equipment and stowed it in the cluttered back seat of the car, I knew I had made a joyful memory which I could also unpack whenever it was required in the future.

After having said farewell to Iain and gone through the hill-day custom of feeding Olive and Mabel al fresco again, we set off on the long drive south. Soon, though, I considered my own hunger and pulled into a cheery-looking truck stop just outside Newtonmore, which I had been assured served very decent food. It was set out in the style of a 1950s American diner with just a couple of lorry drivers in one booth at the end, swearing most impressively without any repetition or deviation as they talked about Rangers and Celtic. Above them a small TV fixed to the wall chirped away and offered the only other entertainment. Then, with the rosy-faced glow and ravenous appetite of the mountains I fell upon my dinner.

As I practically threw my bowl around like Olive at the end of a meal, I decided that this wasn't quite enough and asked the waitress – a young woman from Estonia – if I could please order another fish and chips.

'Something more to drink?'

'No, another fish and chips please.'

You could see that she was still doubtful, wondering if her nascent

English had failed her on this occasion, or maybe that she was still getting to grips with the culture and this was a curious Scottish custom which she hadn't yet experienced, where locals celebrate the arrival of spring by eating a yard of cod.

'Very hungry,' I added unnecessarily, but in a way that I hoped was reassuring. Then, when it arrived, I felt compelled to try and impress by attacking it with the same speed as the first. I realised, as I saw the waiting staff regard me with a blend of curiosity and disgust that my idea of what might impress people has often been wide of the mark.

But it was a strange evening. Two dinners for one person apart, it was just a very normal scene in normal life. Only there was *something* hanging over us – just a feeling that things were not quite right. This oasis of bright, fluorescent lights amidst the darkness outside and the 1950s American diner-style lent it a certain *Twilight Zone* or *Body Snatchers* air and I pretended that I was in one of those stories, where only I could see the truth about the invading horror. I imagined all eyes watching as I paid and left, moving to the door and opening it to the freezing night air, then letting it close behind me as the chatter picked up again – from the staff and the truckers and that television which made itself heard, offering constant news about the coronavirus closing in and growing more serious. It was still background noise but it was getting louder.

Exhausted dogs barely registered my return to the car as we resumed the journey, content with another adventure in the snow and the mountains. It would be the last time we would do so for some time as, for all of us, a very different life was about to begin.

38. Altered Reality

Sometimes I wonder how we got here.

Perhaps I took a bang to the head somewhere early in 2020. Maybe it happened while I was ski-touring on Chno Dearg, trying to avoid a small, blonde dog. Or else I stumbled on my way into the stadium ahead of Wales against Scotland and I currently lie, unconscious, with my snoozing brain concocting all sorts of weird scenarios. Occasionally I think it is the only way to explain the oddness of the world we are all experiencing.

Air travel seems forbidding – a trip away from home for eight weeks now a faintly ridiculous idea. But then, so much of what we did and how we lived pre-coronavirus seems only a half-recalled memory from a lost time and place.

Many things are getting, or will get, back to normal, but others are forever changed. It is as if the world had a collective *Sliding Doors* moment and we took a decision or unwittingly did something which meant that we departed down a side road of reality.

So there is a parallel universe where things go on as before, in more conventional ways, but instead we are now moving down this line – one where we wear masks to buy milk, where mass gatherings carry an unseen threat, where we live and work and meet far more often online than face to face. And also a reality where Tim Rice rewrites the lyrics of 'Don't Cry for Me Argentina' for a couple of Labradors.

I should probably touch upon how perhaps the world's foremost musical lyricist came to tweak one of his greatest works in honour of Olive and Mabel. The connection, of course, was dogs and more specifically Tim's own canine, a boxer called Kirsty. A message popped up on Twitter from the man without whom Andrew Lloyd Webber numbers would still be quite catchy, but just go, 'Dum de dum dum . . .' In fact, part of the message adorns the cover of this book, which was a very kind and generous sentiment and expressed the desire that I should come up with commentary for a video of Kirsty bouncing around in the sea.

'I'll do that one if you add lyrics to these two . . .' was my light-hearted reply, attaching a clip of Olive and Mabel in a field staring at their favourite rubber balls.

And the next morning there it was, a return tweet – 'Written in haste at 1 a.m. for two magnificent hounds' – with an accompanying photo of the new work, titled 'For Mabel and Olive – affectionately'.

It was most odd to receive but also wonderful. So naturally I had to keep my part of the bargain by adding commentary to Kirsty's frolics, with a pay-off line as she soaked her esteemed owner, 'And that's why they wrote about cats instead.' For which Tim was grateful, although he gently pointed out that *Cats* was one musical where he had not worked with Lloyd Webber. But anyway, it was a very nice thing for another dog lover to do and if the actual *Cats* collaborator Trevor Nunn ever gets in touch with a video of his dog, I can reissue my hilarious line.

Meanwhile, the online life of Olive and Mabel continued as I released further videos, or even some little film projects. They seemed to be well enough received, albeit with one or two million views, as opposed to ten or twenty. The viral video moment has passed, but it has been interesting to try and move things on and develop the idea.

Indeed, in terms of development, perhaps the strangest thing was when I received an email from an assistant to one of the foremost figures in the entertainment industry, on either side of the Atlantic. He is a dog lover and a thoroughly nice chap. We talked about ideas for moving things along which was both fascinating and exciting. I said my people would continue to be in touch and left it with Mabel. As a result, we may be waiting some time, but once again the love that people have for dogs helped make a connection.

There were plenty more offers – and not all of them unreasonable. One was suggesting an Olive and Mabel calendar with the dogs in various poses for each month. Another said that they would very much like to go fifty-fifty on a deal where we made T-shirts with a photo of either dog and people would choose their favourites. Or they could sport a slogan or phrase from the videos: 'Mind of a wolf, body of a Care Bear' or 'Tasting absolutely nothing' – ideally, illustrated with a picture of Mabel looking slightly gormless. Somebody from YouTube also offered suggestions as to how to best capitalise on the success of the dogs. Merchandise, or merch, it seems, is a big thing. But it's just not my thing.

Offers from pet agents came in, with a view to Olive and Mabel working in advertisements or becoming social media pet influencers on their own. Much though they (or rather Olive) would be happy to drop me like a sack of potatoes and strike out individually, I felt a little bit protective of them and so turned them down.

Yes, the vast majority of my work had disappeared, but I was still keen to avoid using my dogs as earners in the absence of my usual employment. I could quite easily have viewed my dogs as in a cartoon where they turned, before my avaricious eyes, into dollar signs with ears and a tongue and a wagging tail but I'd rather just have them as they are.

The strangeness kept coming. There was a website set up for this book, but within a day somebody had set up a site which became your unwitting destination if you spelled Mabel incorrectly. One simple mistake would lead you to a place where, instead of discovering the charming talents of my Labradors, you could discover the very different talents of escorts called Olive and 'Mable' – which I have come to accept might not even be their real names.

The dogs themselves were becoming widely recognised. After various TV appearances, their fame was spreading. On a walk a couple of days later, a boy of about ten stared at them as we approached: 'Is this? . . . Are they?? It is! It's Olive and Mabel!' he cried. Then shouted, 'OLIVE AND MABEL OLIVE AND MABEL OLIVE AND MABEL!!!!' to a group of his friends, who came racing over, without the slightest clue what he was talking about but looking keen to be involved.

'Why are they famous?' asked one, who had arrived with his mother.

'Well, they've had millions of people watch them on the internet,' she explained.

'But what do they DO?' he asked, firmly and insistently pursuing this line of inquiry.

'Well . . . they . . .' But she was at a loss. And I couldn't blame her. I couldn't really start to explain it all myself.

I didn't like to say that at that moment they were going through pretty much their entire repertoire. As the group closed in, all demanding selfies, Olive had started to eat grass again and Mabel was looking worried and raising her hackles as a number of small, noisy humans crowded around her. I smoothed down her back while pretending that I was stroking her, like a PR guru concerned about image and worrying that they might all leave muttering 'Wow, that Mabel is a total bitch', even though this would be both accurate and inoffensive to my dogs.

Eventually, after two of them had had pictures taken and Olive had been told by three different children that she was 'a really good boy' I said we had to get going, leaving one particularly distraught youngster in tears as he hadn't got a photo.

'We'll be here again tomorrow!' I said by way of consolation, then a quiet aside to Mabel with a wink: 'Always leave them wanting more . . .' And we walked away with the fur on her back gradually deflating.

The internal dispute I have had is that in a way my relationship with my dogs has changed – and not necessarily for the better. Yes, it is nice to be with them all the time, but how do I see them now? Are they simple commodities; mere actors for whatever the latest project or performance might be? I worry that I have exploited them and perhaps am no different to the Tokyo family dressing their dog up for entertainment. And, nice though it may be for everyone to express their fondness for Olive and Mabel, sometimes I don't feel that I want to share them with anybody else.

Besides, how much longer do you carry on for? In years to come will I be hunting for Olive and Mabel lookalikes to play the same characters, in much the same way that there were several Lassies down the years?

I'm not saying it couldn't work – when I was young my mother had great success in tracking down about seven different goldfish, who I believed were all my original Mr Goldie (who had, in fact lasted no more than a few hours after I won him at a fair), but while I didn't know the truth then, I certainly know the answer now: there is only one Olive and one Mabel and I will always do what's best for them. If that means more filming and chatting for a story or two on social media in the future then that's all good. But if I feel that I or they have had enough and we all just want to curl up in a basket and retire from public life then that will be absolutely fine too. Overwhelmingly, the recent story of Olive and Mabel has been a positive one. From the messages we've had in the strange and strained year of 2020, they have played a real part in keeping people's spirits up, just when it was required.

And in answer to the child's question *that* is what they do – nothing special and yet everything.

39. The Power of the Dog

Let me tell you about a dream I once had. Fear not, I won't keep you long as I am aware that like most of our mind's wanderings while asleep it was largely nonsense and of no interest to anybody else. Whenever I am on the receiving end of these recitals I will quickly step in, informing the dream-teller that I don't really care if they were naked at work one day, or late for an exam, or had the ability to fly, or were staring at an empty grave. During all of which they were also naked.

In fact, it seems that many people were experiencing stranger dreams than usual in 2020, reflecting the oddness and anxiety of life, but this particular dream occurred a couple of years before and was both very simple, needing no interpretation, and also very affecting. In it, I was casually chatting to Olive and she was talking back to me which, in the way of dreams, all seemed perfectly normal – not unlike the ones where I meet Humfrey and don't question the fact that he's about to turn forty. But in this dream, Olive turned to me and said, with a very calm, reassuring tone: 'You do know that I've always loved you.'

As with most dreams it came just before waking and when that happens you carry the feelings created by it into reality for a few moments. But this one stayed with me far longer and left me reasonably emotional, so I headed downstairs, found Olive and wrapped myself around her while she asked just what the *hell* did I think I was doing?

But, of course, the dream wasn't really required. I don't need her to be able to talk to tell me what I already know. We often give dogs far too many human attributes and characteristics – we want to see them in a way that we can relate to and believe they are feeling certain emotions, whereas we may often be a long way wide of the mark. But there are things that you can be certain of without a first-class degree in canine psychology. Yes, there are the overt displays where Olive forgets herself – the welcome at the gate or the morning greeting. But it is the quieter, more subtle instances that tell you more.

So yes, I know what it means when I come in to be met by the tapping of tails on the floor. It's the same thing I know when I'm in another room of an evening and there is a whinny at the door, which is opened to let Olive trot in and curl up in the bed beside my sofa. I know it when she is caught in a quiet reverie, simply staring at me. Yes, her thoughts may often be tangled up with equally strong Labrador feelings of wanting stuff, but I know there is also a deep content – perhaps a sensation of safety and affection. I hear it when she sighs a long, happy exhalation in her bed. I see it when she comes to sit next to me and I feel it when she leans, ever so slightly, against my legs. I just know.

The only problem is that, in relation to our own, dogs seem to be living their lives on fast-forward. Olive is snoozing alongside me now with a little bit of salt sprinkled in the pepper of her chin and flecks of white are scattered across her chest. Every day there seems to be more and every day I have a small moment of sadness as I think about what it means. I can cope far more easily with grey in my own beard than in hers.

While writing this book, news came from Melbourne that Charlie – lovely flat-coated retriever Charlie – one of our surrogate dogs in Australia and greeter after late-night matches at the Australian Open tennis, had gone. No vet was required. He had been struggling for a week or so and had been sick overnight, but hung on until the whole family was up and around him and had said their goodbyes and then he went. His younger assistant Ralph, who worshipped him, was able to go and sniff at his friend, which hopefully helped him come to terms with it. As far as departures go it could have been no better, but it is still a terrible wrench and one which anybody who has owned a dog will know all too well.

Rudyard Kipling wrote a poem called 'The Power of the Dog', which perfectly paints the relationship between human and dog and the pain that comes with all the joy. As an avowed dog lover he could no more cope with the departure of a canine companion than the rest of us and I can't read it without growing rather moist around the eyes:

> When the body that lived at your single will,
> With its whimper of welcome, is stilled (how still!),
> When the spirit that answered your every mood
> Is gone—wherever it goes—for good,
> *You will discover how much you care,*
> *And will give your heart to a dog to tear!*

It is the deal we strike and the pact we make. We know that they are far more likely to leave us than vice versa, but it is an offer which we cannot refuse, because even with the cavernous hole that they leave behind, they bring us far more. In a way they are the daemons of Philip Pullman's His Dark Materials masterpiece – inseparable companions and effectively a part of your soul that, if cut out, leaves you empty.

When I was asked to write this book about my relationship with Olive and Mabel, I took a while to make the decision. I obviously let the prospective publishers know that, despite every sporting event on earth being cancelled I *could* do it but 'would have to try and move a few things around . . .' But then I did have a genuine concern, which was the worrying thought: 'How will I fill a book?' I love my dogs dearly but couldn't necessarily see how explaining that relationship and affection might stretch out more than a couple of pages.

Yet in writing about your dogs you very quickly realise that you are writing about all aspects of your life, because there isn't really a part of it that the dogs don't touch. They entwine themselves around it all – the serious matters and trivial, the fun and the less so. As you have read, they are there for the exciting adventures but also for the mundane. They are with you for everything, and everything is all the better for them.

To return to the viral videos which began all of this, that mass appeal was not down to the mere fact that I had been a sports commentator and was now commentating on any aspect of daily life. I could certainly have worked along those lines and it would have been fine. I could have commentated on a jigsaw being done (yes, this was considered). I could even have had a bash at the Dorset knob-eating contest. But the fact that those videos soared into the stratosphere was down to the simple truth that dogs played the starring roles. Any dog owner who watched will have recognised in Olive and Mabel something of their own companions.

The power of love for dogs is a curious thing. The connection you have with these creatures is so very strong and one that can't really be explained to those who don't share it. But there are millions of people who do. Not that I didn't know it already, but the whole success of Olive and Mabel has shown me just how far-reaching that love for dogs is.

I have spent a great deal of time trying to work out why these creatures have such an effect on us. Perhaps it is their innocence. They have no side or affectation in a world dominated by humans who often move in a very different way. They are our escape, our nearby creatures of trust and love and all such good things. We confide in them and they listen. They empathise even if they might not fully understand. We unburden ourselves and they take it all in. Yes, there might be a bit of greed and I'm not saying that every single one is a saint, but they are at least quite up front about it.

A great number of the messages I have received have been from people who are at various stages of the dog journey. They are thinking of getting a dog, or they are currently deep in puppy love and mayhem. Perhaps they have recently lost their own, or say that our dogs remind them of theirs or even, as quite a few people told me, that they are about to make that heart-wrenching decision to say goodbye. To every owner theirs is the world's best dog and always will be. They are bright rays of sunshine, but the shadow cast is that we will be separated one day and it's almost impossible to think about.

Perhaps one of the strangest aspects of 2020 was one which was not really connected to the Olive and Mabel phenomenon, but rather one that everybody might have experienced – a change in our perception of time. Days and weeks seemed to fly by, with their passage unhindered by events to slow its path. And without those usual events, sporting or otherwise, which are markers and reference points in the year, months and seasons felt unfamiliar. It was all most odd – I even tried to do some reading on the matter to help me better understand it. Although by 'reading' I mean glancing at the theory of relativity on Wikipedia. And by 'understand' I mean looking at it with the same confused expression that Mabel reserves for staring at a bee.

It all gave rise to a feeling of nostalgia in me – partly wishing to be in other days when things might have felt better and safer, partly wanting to grab on to an anchor of the past, as our lives raced by so quickly. Some of that was good, of course – we all wanted to leap forward, to get to the other side of *this* and for things to improve and move on – get back to something approaching the normal life that we had known before. But then I would find myself looking at Olive and Mabel and I so desperately wanted to slam on the brakes – to try and halt the rushing, disappearing days that fall away like cherry blossom.

But let us, in the way of Labradors, be upbeat and optimistic and think more about what dogs bring us than what they leave. Besides, there is a cycle of rebirth with dogs. Not a literal reincarnation, but no matter how much you love one single dog, another can appear and take over the vital task performed entirely unwittingly but oh-so reliably – to give us love and to receive it and to help steer us through this strange world. We will always hold on to the memories of the ones we have had but also let another come in, one who will pick things up as if to say, 'It's okay . . . it's my turn now.' And *that* is the real power of a dog.

So, in Melbourne, Charlie has a successor in a yellow Labrador retriever called Ollie, with Ralph now in the unfamiliar role of senior partner in the firm – very probably promoted above his talents. Charlie is not replaced and never forgotten, but Ollie is just the next in line. The new occupant of a junior, but very important, position.

In fact, Caroline took me rather by surprise recently as she said, 'Do you think we should get another dog?'

It was the first time it had seriously been considered. Perhaps she was thinking of enlarging the supporting cast for future videos, although that has a certain air of Scrappy-Doo being added to the ensemble and, if we're honest, he was just annoying. But, if (and clearly I mean when) a new arrival does come along I have no doubt that she will burrow her way into our lives and our hearts – like all the dogs we have had before, like the very special two we have now and like all those we will surely have in years to come.

Epilogue

'Head down and keep going . . . Just think of Yuichiro Miura.' My father took a pause and leaned on his walking pole, as if giving the advice some consideration, but also recognising a chance for another breather.

'Who's that then?' he asked, through a swig of water.

'Yuichiro Miura. Japanese bloke. Became the oldest person to climb Everest when he got up there aged eighty. Took the record from a 76-year-old Sherpa. So, what I'm *saying* is that he was three years older than you are now when he made it to the roof of the world and that, basically, 2,800 feet of Scottish hill should be a breeze.'

We were on the upper slopes of the Merrick – a big, rounded lump in the south-western corner of Scotland and the highest point of the Southern Uplands. It was so often visible from Troon, growing up, but I had never got round to climbing it as there were so many more appealing mountains to the north. Now it seemed ideal, close at hand and offering a chance to catch up with my dad. Post-lockdown, it was a time for seeing family again and trying to move closer to some sort of normality.

I hadn't spoken to him for a few weeks, perhaps even a month or two. Or three. I should explain that this does not mean some cataclysmic falling out – it's just our way. Plenty of father-son relationships will be far more openly emotional with regular back-slapping hugs and expressions of manly love and pride. As expert practitioners of Scottish male repression, we prefer to do our own thing, then every few months get together for a hill walk and lay bare our innermost feelings with a brief chat about Scotland's chances in the rugby.

The more demonstrative Olive and Mabel were both panting away in the sunshine and looking as happy and hopeful as ever, firmly believing that every stop should lead to snacks. At this moment, my dad looked neither of these things, but did seem to be giving my advice some serious thought. And his response was both considered and fair.

'Bugger off . . .'

'Only trying to help,' I said, as I stretched back my shoulders under the straps of the rucksack and continued my way up the path, deciding that now was the time to add some extra detail. 'So the Sherpa – a guy called Min Bahadur Sherchan – *he* then tried to take back the record, aged 85, but ended up dying at Base Camp, which wasn't ideal. Then there was Brian Blessed – I think he was in his sixties when he made his last attempt. Got to over 25,000 feet in 1996 – of course that was the year of the disaster when eight people died in a storm . . . They made a film of it with Jake Gyllenhaal . . . Not great as I recall.'

I realised that my motivational speech had rather lost its way. And, in fact, I noticed that I had also lost my audience, as my dad had stayed in place, looking out at the view which we had earned in two thousand feet of climbing. Olive was still with him and I was now lecturing only Mabel – and one thing she does not require is added motivation. Indeed, at that moment she was bounding through the heather – partly for her own enjoyment, partly to ensure a most thorough tick inspection later on. So I decided to do my own thing for a bit, push on and wait for them further ahead.

This was my second trip to the hills after months of effective house-arrest, but it felt as if it deserved to be the first. Part of the problem with my original escape was that it had been an ideal which lived in my head and, fed by all that time and all the events which took place, it grew into an epic. I could see it all – glorious new photos of Olive and Mabel at the top of another mountain. Instagram get ready, it was going to be perfect. But in the end, the whole trip was horrendous.

At the end of July, Iain Cameron and I had decided to try and get sunrise on Beinn Trilleachan, by Loch Etive, just south of Glen Coe, with an overnight camp on the summit. It sounded ideal, but the reality was different – crowds and litter by the loch, midges descending in spiteful clouds and a weather forecast which, we real-ised as we climbed, had been so enormously incorrect that I fully expected the head of the Met Office to be resigning at a tear-filled press conference the next day.

With cold, sleety rain driving in on the summit ridge, the decision to abandon was easily taken. It was then a soul-destroying, ankle-turning descent, including an ill-advised diversion through forestry land which resulted in Iain having to throw both dogs to me over a fence, with Olive landing safely, claws-first, on my face.

Never have two people packed up and left so quickly – partly to avoid death by a thousand midge bites, but more importantly to be done with the whole episode.

Now, nearly two months later, it was very different. The sky was clear and autumn had crept in – even in Scotland where the seasons can struggle to separate, it is a time of year so easily recognisable without knowing exactly why. Perhaps that cooler edge of the air, the smell of damp, tilled earth, or the light a shade softer than high summer. However you define it, the season which, more than any other, prompts contemplation was with us. I could see my dad a couple of hundred yards behind with Olive still there for company, so I untangled Mabel from my legs and kept moving.

I was thinking about my own stage in life. I had recently been told that forty-seven is, apparently, a most significant age. Somebody with several degrees – or just a loud voice and confident manner – had worked out that it is the definitive point of middle-age, where you reach the crossroads of life. From this junction you either carry straight on, or you branch off in a different direction and see what you find.

Well, perhaps the theory was right after all as, for a couple of years, I had been wondering if I should try something else. Not that I don't love my job – I do, and hope and expect to be broadcasting on sport for years to come. But there was always just a feeling that there might be *more* out there.

Lots of people will be familiar with that feeling, or something similar – you bounce into a job as a youngster and you enjoy it, life keeps on rolling as you pass the markers and milestones of perhaps buying a house, moving upwards in your career, starting a family or even getting a dog. Then you realise that middle-age has somehow occurred and for the first time you pause, to look around and take stock.

I had often thought that I might like to do something different, although my desire had been that unsure-about-exactly-what kind of desire, a lack of clarity combined with a middle-aged lack of energy that makes getting up from the sofa of an evening quite a momentous decision, let alone starting afresh with an entire career change. So I was looking vaguely over in another direction, but at what, I didn't really know. Perhaps writing, comedy, making programmes – something creative, something . . . *else*.

Then 2020 happened and I did find myself making a turn. Or rather, circumstances had eased me gently down a side road, with the potential to go further if I wanted. Forced to keep busy with anything, this awful year provided the motivation and necessity to try something new. If you are dithering and wondering, it can definitely help to be given a push.

And it so happened that I had just turned forty-seven. In fact, I did so on the day of midges and misery on Trilleachan. Now I reached the broad summit of the Merrick with three-year-old Mabel – who, as far as I'm aware, had no important life decisions to make – and a few minutes later the elder human and dog joined us.

There we broke out our sandwiches by the enormous, tumble-down cairn, sipped our coffee and took it all in: Ailsa Craig rising out of the Firth of Clyde with the sun slipping down towards the Isle of Arran. In the west there was the very faintest blue-grey outline of the Mull of Kintyre, and further still Northern Ireland and the Antrim coast. To the south, you could see England and the distant peaks of the Lake District – everywhere you looked, a prospect.

This was no wild and isolated place – civilisation was not too far away, but up here we seemed, at last, so far from all the chatter and pace of the world – above everything that had happened in those unsettling months of 2020.

Somewhere down there life continued – news and events and problems and issues. People working and sharing and agreeing or arguing, with everything no doubt racing by at an uncanny speed. But up here everything slowed and was quiet and still. It is rare to find that total silence in our world, so take as much in when you can. Breathe deeply.

My other therapy was wandering around nearby, in their near-constant state of truffling with expert snouts. In a year when everybody has had their mental health sorely tested, I'm not entirely sure how I would have coped without Olive and Mabel – I only know that 2020 would have been far harder. Dogs offer comfort in a troubling time, for whoever keeps them, whoever feeds them, for whoever they walk alongside. That's certainly been the case for me with Olive and Mabel and, at a time when we were *all* feeling the strain, they performed that duty for so many other people as well. Apart from anything else, they have given me something to concentrate on when so much else had fallen away. In a very literal sense, I'm not sure what I would have done without them.

However, dogs rarely sit and contemplate life and sometimes it might be better for us to function that way. We dwell on the past and fret about the future while they think only of this moment. So the quiet and my pondering was broken by a questioning whine from Mabel – although her 'What are we doing here?' seemed less philosophical and more that she had simply forgotten.

'Shall we get going?' said my dad.

'I'm just going to finish my drink,' I replied. 'Incidentally . . .' I went on, digging in my rucksack for another bit of chocolate and a pair of gloves, '. . . there was a woman from Edinburgh called Elsa Yates who finished her third round of all the Munros at the age of seventy-six. So just have a think about that – plenty of mountains still to . . .'

But when I looked up he had wisely made the decision to go and I was left talking only to my dogs again. Which, I suppose, is where all of this began.

If this were some sort of crossroads then I still don't know in which direction I, or we, are heading. So much has changed for us – yes, for Olive, Mabel and me, but really for everyone. It is the uncertainty of the world now that shakes us, but the unknown can also be exciting. The story unwritten. The peaks unclimbed.

So we'll leave you where we started, on top of a hill with Olive and Mabel, with plenty more days ahead for us and many more things yet to do. I heave my rucksack on to my shoulders and we set off in our familiar formation – me in front, Olive sniffing the ground and following at her own pace, while Mabel skips around, mouth open, tongue sticking out and getting in the way.

'Come on then . . .' I say. And, with a scratch behind the ears, I make sure to tell them – just one more time – what very good dogs they are.

Acknowledgements

Thanks . . .

To Caroline, for joint dog custody and all other things.

To everyone at Black & White Publishing for steering a novice through uncharted waters.

Also to all at Text Publishing for their nurturing ways in Australia and New Zealand.

To Tom Fordyce – occasional running partner for Olive and seasoned campaigner in the world of writing for his advice.

To Iain Cameron, snow expert and also expert mountain dog-photographer.

To Tim Rice for allowing us to feature his kind words in a position of some prominence (and for rewriting a fairly successful musical).

To anybody who watched and enjoyed the videos which began all this and even more gratitude to those who have read this book.

To Don Wargowsky for taking both mountains and dog care to the extreme and for telling his story.

To Henry and Bisto and Rocky and Izzy, for getting together all those years ago.

And of course, to their offspring, Olive and Mabel, who have contributed absolutely nothing and yet also everything to this book and our lives.